Transforming Social Work Practice

Reflective Reader
Social Work and Human Development

Karin Crawford

Learning Matters

First published in 2006 by Learning Matters Ltd.

British Library Cataloguing in Publication Data
A CIP record for this book is available from the British Library.

ISBN-10: 1 84445 050 3
ISBN-13: 978 1 84445 050 3

Cover design by del norte (Leeds) Ltd
Project management by Deer Park Productions, Tavistock, Devon
Typeset by PDQ Typesetting Ltd
Printed and bound in Great Britain by Bell & Bain Ltd, Glasgow

Learning Matters Ltd
33 Southernhay East
Exeter EX1 1NX
Tel: 01392 215560
Email: info@learningmatters.co.uk
www.learningmatters.co.uk

Contents

Acknowledgements

I would like to thank Sarah for her time, patience and constructive feedback in working through many of the activities and the reflective exercises as this book was being written. Thanks also to colleagues at the University of Lincoln, especially Janet Walker, for assisting me to find time to write this book and finally to Dai whose continual support has made this possible.

Introduction

The series

The *Reflective Readers* series supports the *Transforming Social Work Practice* series by providing relevant and topical theory and research that underpins the reflective learning and practice of social work students.

Each book includes extracts from classic and current publications and documents. These extracts are supported by analysis, pre- and post-reading activities, links to the National Occupational Standards, academic benchmarks and social work values, a practical implications section, links to other titles in the *TSWP* series and suggestions for further reading.

Integrating theory and practice, the *Reflective Reader* series is specifically designed to encourage students to develop the skill and habit of reflecting on their own practice, engaging with relevant theory and identifying opportunities to apply theory to improve their professional practice.

In this series, the emphasis is on theory and research. The authors guide the student to analyse practice within a theoretical framework provided by a range of texts. Through examining *why* we do *what* we do and *how* we do it, the reader will be able to relate theory to practice. In this way, the series promotes the development of evidence-based practice in social work. The series will cover the core subject areas of the social work degree.

Each book provides focused coverage of subjects and topics and each extract is accompanied by support material to help students and lecturers to engage with the extract, draw out the implications for professional practice and to develop as a reflective practitioner.

Whilst the series is aimed principally at students, as practitioners return to undertake the new range of post-qualifying awards in social work, they are likely to turn to these texts to refresh and update their knowledge.

Each book includes guidance, advice and examples on:

- the knowledge, understanding, theory and practice needed to meet the national occupational standards and academic benchmarks;
- how to relate knowledge, theory and practice to a course of study;
- self reflection and analysis through personal responses and reading alone;
- developing approaches to sharing views with fellow students.

Readers will develop their skills in relating theory to practice through:

- preparatory reading;
- analysis;
- personal responses;
- practical implications and activities;
- further reading.

Human Growth and Development

The National Occupational Standards for Social Work, Key Role 6 requires social workers to 'demonstrate professional competence in social work practice' through research, analysis, evaluation and the use of current knowledge of best social work practice. Additionally the General Social Care Council Codes of Practice for Social Care Workers state that social care workers must be accountable for the quality of their work and take responsibility for maintaining and improving their knowledge and skills.

This reflective reader has been written for social work students and registered social work practitioners. It aims to assist social work students, particularly those who are towards the end of their undergraduate studies, to meet the national requirements and to provide a mechanism for qualified social workers to evidence professional development and work towards meeting the 'Post Registration Training and Learning' requirements for maintenance of their registration. The five core areas of knowledge as identified for social work students by the Department of Health will be integrated in the chapters of the book, with Human Growth and Development being the key focus.

This book will support and develop the concepts explored in other texts in the series, in particular, Crawford and Walker (2003) *Social work and human development.* This will be achieved through the provision of relevant, topical theory and research to underpin reflective learning and practice. Thus the book draws upon extracts from key classics as well as contemporary publications, legislation, guidance and policy upon which to base critical analysis, case studies, further reading and reader activities that will enable the reader to develop their ability to integrate and apply knowledge in practice and reflect upon their experiences. In this way readers are given the opportunity to develop as research-minded, evidence-based practitioners.

This reflective reader makes explicit links to the National Occupational Standards for social work and the emerging post-qualifying framework for social work.

NB Where references are quoted within an extract, they do not appear in the reference section at the back of the book but should be sought from the original source.

Author

Karin Crawford is a senior lecturer at the University of Lincoln, School of Health and Social Care. In this role she has responsibility for supporting learners, teaching and curriculum development in the area of health, social care and management both at undergraduate and post-qualifying levels. Karin also has experience of working with other European countries to develop teaching and learning in health and social care. Additionally, Karin is part of a transnational research project which aims to address social exclusion and poverty as it relates to single parent families and their children. Prior to joining the university, Karin gained substantial practice experience in both health and social care, firstly as a registered nurse and later as a qualified social worker and manager. This experience has spanned statutory, voluntary and private sector and has included general nursing, social work, policy development and the management of both adult and children's care management services. Karin has co-authored two previous texts in the *Transforming Social Work Practice Series*; *Social Work and Human Development* (2003) and *Social Work and Older People* (2004).

Series Editor

Professor Jonathan Parker is Head of Social Work and Learning Disability at Bournemouth University, UK and, with colleagues, has developed the Centre for Social Work and Social Care Research. He is co-editor of the highly successful Transforming Social Work Practice series and has published widely in social work education, practice learning, theories of social work and dementia and palliative care, including ten books and over 50 journal articles. He is a past chair of the Association of Teachers in Social Work Education and current vice-chair of the Joint University Council Social Work Education Committee in the UK. He is currently engaged in research into effectiveness in practice learning.

Acknowledgements

Grewal et al, *Making the transition: addressing barriers in services for disabled people.* Department for Work and Pensions **www.dwp.gov.uk**. © Crown Copyright. Reprinted by permission of the Department for Work and Pensions; Godfrey, Mary, Townsend, Jean and Denby, Tracy, *Building a good life for older people in local communities: the experience of ageing in time and place*, 2004 The Joseph Rowntree Foundation. Reproduced by permission of the Joseph Rowntree Foundation; Jones, Gill, *The youth divide: diverging paths to adulthood* 2002 The Joseph Rowntree Foundation. Reproduced by permission of the Joseph Rowntree Foundation; Mills, Chris, *Problems at home, problems at school.* © Copyright (2004) NSPCC; Grant et al. (eds), *Learning Disability: A life cycle approach to valuing people*, 2005. Reproduced with kind permission of the Open University Press/McGraw-Hill Publishing Company; Permissions c/o Palgrave Macmillan 175 Fifth Avenue New York, NY 10010; Moon, Jenny, *Handbook of Reflective and Experimental Learning,* (©2004) RoutledgeFalmer. Reproduced by permission of Taylor & Francis Books UK; Eamon, Mary Keegan, 'The Effects of Poverty on Children's Socioemotional Development; An Ecological Systems Analysis'. © Copyright 2001, National Association of Social Workers, Inc, Social Work; Morss, J. R. 'The several social constructions of James, Jenks and Prout: A contribution to the sociological theorization of childhood' *The International Journal of Children's Rights 10* (2002). Reproduced by permission of Koninklijke Brill NV; Calder, A. and Cope, R., 'Breaking Barriers' from *Reaching the Hardest to Reach* (March 2004). Reprinted by permission of The Prince's Trust; Woodhead, M and Montgomery, H *Understanding Childhood: an interdisciplinary approach* (2003). Copyright John Wiley & Sons Limited. Reproduced with permission.

Achieving post-qualifying social work awards

At the beginning of each chapter, you will be shown which of the National Occupational Standards for Social Work, key roles and units, can be met within that chapter. However, the following values and ethics from the National Occupational Standards for Social Work relate to the whole text and are given below:

Values and ethics

a.   Awareness of your own values, prejudices, ethical dilemmas and conflicts of interest and their implications on your practice.

b.   Respect for, and the promotion of:
   – each person as an individual;
   – independence and quality of life for individuals, whilst protecting them from harm;
   – dignity and privacy of individuals, families, carers, groups and communities.

d.   Value, recognise and respect the diversity, expertise and experience of individuals, families, carers, groups and communities.

f.   Understand and make use of strategies to challenge discrimination, disadvantage and other forms of inequality and injustice.

If you are a registered social worker, this book will also assist you to evidence post-registration training and learning. It relates to the post-qualifying framework for social work education and training national criteria at the *specialist* level, in particular:

(ii) Think critically about their own practice in the context of the GSCC codes of practice, national and international codes of professional ethics and the principles of diversity, equality and social inclusion in a wide range of situations, including those associated with inter-agency and inter-professional work.

(iv) Draw on knowledge and understanding of service users' and carers' issues to actively contribute to strategies and practice which promote service users' and carers' rights and participation in line with the goals of choice, independence and empowerment.

(v) Use reflection and critical analysis to continuously develop and improve their specialist practice, including their practice in interprofessional and inter-agency contexts, drawing systematically, accurately and appropriately on theories, models and relevant up-to-date research.

(vi) Extend initial competence so as to develop in-depth competence in the context of one area of specialist practice to agreed national specialist standards, drawing on knowledge and experience of the range of settings and service systems that impact on the lives of service users.

Additionally, Chapter 7 specifically enables you to:

(ix) Take responsibility for the effective use of supervision to identify and explore issues, develop and implement plans and improve own practice.

In addition, chapters 2, 3 and 4 relate specifically to the Specialist Standards and Requirements for Post Qualifying Social Work Education and Training in respect of Children, Young People, their Families and Carers, in particular, 'Promoting the development of children and young people and helping to meet additional or complex needs'.

These chapters also relate to the Common Core of Skills and Knowledge for the Children's Workforce, specifically the area of expertise titled 'Child and Young Person Development'.

1 Human life course development and social work practice

Introduction

This first chapter aims to provide an introduction to the rest of the book in three different ways: by explaining the purpose, structure and function of this reflective reader; by exploring some of the more significant terms and potential definitions that may be helpful as you use this book; and finally, by giving a broad overview of different ways in which human life course development can be perceived and understood.

How to use this book

This book is separated into seven chapters, the title of each chapter clearly indicating the chapter focus. This first chapter and the final chapter adopt a different structure to the five chapters between. This chapter has three sections as detailed above, whilst Chapter 7 focuses on assisting you to identify ways in which you might use the learning achieved through your studies with this text. In that final chapter you will also be encouraged to look at how you might progress your learning further, in terms of both the areas or topics to explore and the types of study that you might undertake. Within this, the importance of keeping records of your learning, your reflections, your progress through this text and the impact this learning has had upon your professional development and practice, are highlighted, and you will read about ways in which you can record and share learning, using the skills of critical analysis, reflection and synthesis.

Chapters 2 to 6 provide relevant and topical policy, legislation, theory and research extracts to inform and stimulate your reflective learning about human development across the life course and its significance to informed social work practice. Chapters 2 and 3 should be studied together as they examine development across the early and middle years of childhood. Chapter 4 moves further through the life course and explores the ways in which people develop through the adolescent period of their lives. Chapters 5 and 6 then relate to development in adulthood, with Chapter 6 specifically looking at later adulthood.

Each of these core chapters contains three sections, which are framed around key reflective questions. These questions, given at the start of each section, are offered as a mechanism by which you might stimulate your reflective juices! In other words, they act as prompts or starting points to assist your thinking around the topic. Within each section you are then guided towards texts that you should read, or have a broad knowledge of, as contextual materials, before embarking on the analysis of the extract that follows. Most usually within these chapters, the pre-reading suggestions are publicly available documents detailing strategy, policy or law, often accessed easily through the Internet. The extracts within each section are relevant to the life course period and topic of that chapter section and can be seen to be informative in respect of social work practice. A brief analysis of key messages within that extract is then presented, followed by suggestions for activities that you might undertake, not only to further and deepen your learning in that particular respect, but also to ensure that you continually relate your learning to its influence on your social work practice.

Finally, at the end of each chapter, I have provided some suggestions for further reading and research, with brief annotations about the texts, organisations and Internet website addresses given.

Whilst the book takes a *whole of life approach,* it sets out to be a *reflective reader* and, as such, it does not claim to be able to explore every facet of human development across the life course, or every element of social work practice. More accurately, the content of the chapters, the pre-reading suggestions, the policy, legislation and research extracts, the analysis offered and the personal reflective activities aim to provide prompts and signposts to stimulate your reflections, facilitate your learning and indicate areas for further study.

As you read and study the different elements of this book, you will identify a number of themes or threads that are integrated throughout the text. These themes, listed below, are directly relevant to social work practice underpinned by knowledge and understanding of a whole-of-life approach to human development.

Individual and collective identities

This theme refers to the tension between the different identities that we hold for ourselves or that are perceived or 'given' to us, by others. Whilst this is a theme throughout the book, it is particularly relevant to discussion in Chapter 4, where the importance of both individual difference and identity as a young person, and the collective social identity as an adolescent, or a teenager, is considered.

Continuity and change

The notion of continuity and change can also be found throughout this text. Continuity refers to expectations, lifelong development and progression through the life course, whilst change is often characterised by life events, or transitions. However, whilst continuity and change might be perceived to be opposites, in the life course they are intrinsically related. In Chapter 5 of this book, for example, you will read about how disabled adults experience transitions and the particular issues that specific transitions may raise for continuity and changes in their life course.

Similarity and difference

The discussion raised by this theme can be seen to reflect many of the issues that the notions of individual and collective identities may raise. As you read through this reflective reader, particularly as you read the extracts and pre-reading suggestions, consider how far individual and collective similarities and differences have been taken into account. Then, perhaps even more fundamentally, consider how far it is desirable that either individual or collective, similarities and differences are accounted for. This could, with your colleagues or peers, allow for some stimulating, if heated, debate! In Chapter 4, I refer to the work of Michele A Paludi (2002) who explores, through a number of selected readings, *Human development in multicultural contexts* (Paludi, 2002). Paludi's work offers insight into particular areas of difference, in that it offers a multicultural perspective and reminds us that *integrating the scholarship on race, sex, ethnicity, and class into research on life-cycle developmental psychology adds an important dimension: It provides more understanding of the development of **all** people* (Paludi, 2002, page 8 – emphasis added).

Equilibrium and instability

This theme has much in common with the other tensions discussed above. As with continuity and change it may appear that equilibrium and instability are at two different ends of a continuum, whereas 'in reality' people often experience these two processes at the same time in their lives. For example, the life event known as retirement, which is explored in Chapter 6, is frequently characterised by instability, change and loss, but this may at the same time, be associated with appreciation of the stability and equilibrium found in the family, the community, and the expansion of opportunities that may become available.

The narrative approach

This is discussed further in the next section of this chapter.

As you study the materials in the chapters, you could highlight where each of these themes is apparent to you. You will find that there are sections where I have made this explicit, but there are many others where these issues, debates or themes are more implicit in the discussion.

Understanding terms and definitions

Many words, terms or phrases have contestable, debateable or alternate meanings, particularly some of those that health and social care practitioners use in their everyday professional lives. In an attempt to establish clarity within this text, I have provided a short glossary of terms and abbreviations at the end of the book, as it is important that you read and understand the text within the context and meaning in which it was written.

However, there are two key terms, used throughout the text, that would benefit from some discussion and clarification at this point in this introductory chapter: *a life course perspective*; and the *narrative approach*.

A life course perspective

Runyan (cited in Sugarman, 2001) provides the definition of life course as:

> The sequence of events and experiences in a life from birth until death, and the chain of personal states and encountered situations which influence, and are influenced by this sequence of events. (Sugarman, 2001, page 11)

This reflective reader encourages you to take a life course perspective, not only as you study human life course development, but in all aspects of your professional practice.

This means that you perceive the whole of life, from conception to death, as being a progressive, developmental path along which there are always opportunities for growth and change across all life's facets. The consequence of taking a life course perspective for your developing social work practice is that, as you work with service users, you will aim to understand their circumstances as individuals who have travelled on their very personal life course pathways, and been influenced by their unique experiences and trajectory.

The narrative approach

In the next section of the chapter you will read about the range of different ways in which development across the life course can be understood. Sugarman (2001) suggests that *the life course as a narrative construction* is one of the ways of explaining life course development. This means that the stories people tell about their own lives, the personal meaning that they attach to their stories and their development of self-identity is, in itself, a way of understanding human development.

In this book, however, I have used the term narrative approach in a more functional way to describe *a way of working with individuals that focuses on the importance of their own first-hand account of their life, their experiences and the meaning they attach to them* (Crawford and Walker, 2003, page 3). The narrative approach is also sometimes referred to as a life story, biographical or life history approach. In essence, these terms have the same meaning, although in different texts authors may attach differing emphases on particular aspects of these ways of working. Hockey and James (2003) focus on the development of personal and social identities through the course of an individual's life. They refer to life histories as mechanisms through which to study social life and suggest that *a coherent and explanatory narrative is carved out of a set of diverse experiences and a set of past identities and assembled to account for a present identity* (Hockey and James, 2003, page 210).

Parker and Bradley (2003, page 57), however, make the direct connection between the narrative approach and social work practice in considering how using *life road maps* with service users can provide an illustration of significant life events as perceived by the individual service user. Life road maps are just one social work practice tool that may contribute to the construction of a detailed social work assessment that takes a narrative approach. As well as a tool to aid social work processes, the construction of our own narrative, or story, is described by Sugarman (2001, page 174) as a therapeutic tool that can raise our self-esteem and help us to construct our identities. It can be seen, therefore, that, as set out in the opening paragraph of this section, Sugarman's argument that *narrative construction* is, in itself, a theory of life course, can be seen to be accurate, in that by taking this approach to working with individuals, you will be enabling them to theorise their own life course and to develop their own understanding of their circumstances. Further examples of narrative or biographical approaches within social work practice are given throughout this book, particularly in Chapter 5, where person-centred approaches to working with people with learning disabilities are examined.

Different approaches to understanding human life course development

There are many different ways in which human growth and development across the life course can be perceived and understood. In this book you will be introduced to some of them and will be given the opportunity to critique them and the ways in which these different approaches impact upon social work practice. For example, in Chapter 3, you will take an ecological systems approach to life course development to examine how poverty may affect a child's development. This approach suggests that development is dependent upon the interaction between the person and their environment. In Chapter 5, when studying development in adulthood, you will look at how life course development can be understood as a progressive series of stages, which are often age-related. Another way of understanding the life course is to view it as a sequence of life events or transitions. In Chapter 6, for example, this perspective on life course is explored through an analysis of significant changes and transitions in later adulthood, in particular, retirement. Typically these different approaches to explaining and understanding how people grow and develop over the course of their lives arise from emphasis on different aspects or dimensions of human life. Examples of aspects that might be focused upon include physical, or biological development (this is considered, for example, in Chapter 2); social, interpersonal development; cognitive development (examined further in Chapter 3); psychological development; and emotional development.

In this book, whilst encouraging you to develop your understanding of a wide range of approaches to understanding life course development, I would suggest that human development is complex and multifaceted. The influential theory of development put forward by Paul Baltes (1987, cited in Crawford and Walker, 2003) captures the complexity, individuality and fluidity of a life course perspective. Baltes' *Theoretical proposition of life-span development psychology* stated that:

- human development is *multidimensional*;
- human development is *multidirectional*;
- human development is *plastic* (flexible, changeable and may take many paths);
- human development is *culturally and historically embedded*;
- human development is *contextual* (dependent upon how the person responds and interacts with everything around them).

As you study the different sections of the chapters with this book, you could keep Baltes' ideas in your mind, so that you can develop your own ideas about whether his approach is helpful in explaining how we develop across our lives.

Chapter summary

This introductory chapter and Chapter 7, the final chapter of this book, provide the 'bread and butter' to frame the more substantial and specific chapters that go between them, to make this 'reflective sandwich'! This chapter has set out the purpose and structure of this reader and has given an overview of different perspectives on human life course development and how they are discussed within the book. The final chapter, which it may be helpful to look through before more detailed study on individual chapters, provides ideas about how to develop as a reflective practitioner through your studies with this book and beyond. The ideas and processes that are developed in Chapter 7 underpin the whole purpose and function of this reflective reader. I hope that you enjoy your reading and studies of this text and that it successfully facilitates and stimulates your appetite for further learning.

2 Early childhood development

ACHIEVING A SOCIAL WORK DEGREE

This chapter will begin to help you to meet the following National Occupational Standards:

Key Role 1: Prepare for, and work with, individuals, families, carers, groups and communities to assess their needs and circumstances.
- Prepare for social work contact and involvement.
- Assess needs and options to make a recommended course of action.

Key Role 2: Plan, carry out, review and evaluate social work practice, with individuals, families, carers, groups, communities and other professionals.
- Interact with individuals, families, carers, groups and communities to achieve change and development and to improve life opportunities.
- Work with groups to promote individual growth, development and independence.

Key Role 5: Manage and be accountable, with supervision and support, for your own social work practice within your organisation.
- Work within multi-disciplinary and multi-organisational teams, networks and systems.

Key Role 6: Demonstrate professional competence in social work practice.
- Research, analyse, evaluate, and use current knowledge of best social work practice.

It will also introduce you to the following academic standards as set out in the social work subject benchmark statement:

3.1.1 Social work services and service users
- The nature and validity of different definitions of, and explanations for, the characteristics and circumstances of service users and the services required by them.

3.1.2 The service delivery context
- The complex relationships between public, social and political philosophies, policies and priorities and the organisation and practice of social work, including the contested nature of these.
- The significance of legislative and legal frameworks and service delivery standards.

3.1.3 Values and ethics
- The nature, historical evolution and application of social work values.

3.1.4 Social work theory

- The relevance of psychological and physiological perspectives to understanding individual and social development and functioning.
- Models and methods of assessment, including factors underpinning the selection and testing of relevant information, the nature of professional judgement and the processes of risk assessment.

3.2.2. Problem solving skills
3.2.2.2 Gathering information
3.2.2.3 Analysis and synthesis

Introduction

This chapter and the chapter that follows focus on human development through child-hood in contemporary British society. Whilst, as you will read within the various chapters of this book and the recommended texts, human development cannot be simplified and effectively categorised into age-related segments, it has been necessary to divide and define childhood, using age, in order to provide structure and coherence to this text. Thus, Chapter 2 will explore development of infants and young children from birth to about five years old, with Chapter 3 concentrating on the middle years of childhood from five years to approximately 12 years of age. The two chapters should be viewed as one chapter, in two parts. As there are so many different aspects of development that influence a child's experiences and growth, it is not possible to cover them all in both chapters. Therefore, in this chapter, you will consider the broad concept of childhood in our society, before examining physical and emotional develop-ment in early childhood. In the final section of this chapter you will explore the way in which issues of safety, security and stability may impact upon development in early childhood. Then, as you progress to Chapter 3, you will look at cognitive development and psychological development in childhood. In Chapter 3, you will also consider how children's views and experiences are heard and the influence that increasing self-confi-dence and self-esteem may have on childhood development. Your studies of Chapter 3 will also engage you in consideration of the impact of deprivation and poverty on devel-opment in childhood. Thus, across both chapters, you will have the opportunity to read about and reflect upon your understanding of physical, cognitive, emotional, social and personal development through childhood.

The structure of the chapters, whilst not intended to be so, could be seen to reflect the significance that our society puts upon different aspects of growth during childhood. So, for example, when considering the development of babies and toddlers, profes-sionals, parents, carers and lay people often focus upon physical growth targets, or milestones. Yet in the middle years of childhood the focus is more likely to be on academic and social development.

Chapters 2 and 3 have been written to enable you to learn about and reflect upon child-hood development and social work within the context of national contemporary policy and strategy. In accordance with the government green paper *Every child matters* (DfES, 2003) a set of common skills, knowledge and values for all people who work with children, young people and their families has been developed. *Child and young person development* is one area that is highlighted within the *Common core of skills and knowledge* document set out by the Department for Education and Skills (DfES, 2005a, page 10). The green paper, *Every child matters* (DfES, 2003) identifies five key outcomes that are considered to be the most important to children and young people (see Fig. 2.1):

- be healthy
- stay safe
- enjoy and achieve
- make a positive contribution
- achieve economic well-being.

These five outcomes are also at the heart of the Children Act 2004, which provides the legal conduit for the green paper and the accompanying strategic development programme *Every child matters: Change for children* (DfES, 2004) (**www.every childmatters.gov.uk**). Each of the five outcomes provides the focus for a section in this, or the next, chapter and is used to facilitate discussion and reflections about what these mean for different aspects of childhood development. Throughout both chapters you will be encouraged to read sections of the green paper and related policy documents in order to assist you to contextualise childhood development and related social work practice within present-day society.

In this chapter, the first two of the five key outcomes for children are addressed: *being healthy* and *staying safe*. Within this, reflective questions are raised to help you to:

- consider how the meanings attached to childhood influence development and impact upon how childhood is experienced;
- evaluate explanations of how children develop physically and emotionally in early childhood; and
- understand the significance of safety, security and stability for early childhood development.

The final three outcomes provide the three sections in Chapter 3: *enjoying and achieving; making a positive contribution;* and *achieving economic well-being*. The 'outcomes framework' published in *Every child matters: Change for children* (DfES, 2004) provides not only the five key outcomes, but also related aims for children. These are reproduced diagrammatically in Fig. 2.1, to give you an overview of all the outcomes and aims.

Throughout this chapter and the next, a selection of extracts from theoretical texts and recent research findings is provided to enable you to reflect on the implications of the policy direction and the ways in which research and knowledge are integrated and assimilated into policy and practice in social work. It is suggested that you work through Chapters 2 and 3 systematically, undertaking the activities, making notes and recording your reflections and responses as you progress. It is advisable to record your learning through these chapters, in order to collate evidence of your continuing professional development and your commitment to best social work practice. Further guidance and advice on different ways in which to record and share your learning are given in Chapter 7 of this book.

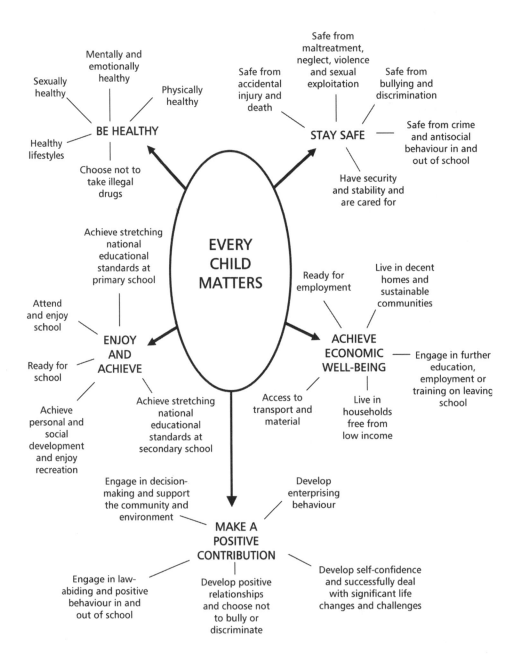

Figure 2.1 Extract from 'outcomes framework'

Adapted from Every child matters: Change for children (DFES, 2004)

Social construction of childhood

As an introduction to your study of childhood development, through the rest of this chapter and Chapter 3, this first section encourages you to reflect upon what childhood means in our society. Here I introduce some of the core concepts and hypotheses, in relation to the period of human life known as *childhood*, that you need to understand before studying further. The reflective questions that you should consider as you read through this section of the chapter are:

- How do I interpret and understand the concept of childhood, in respect of my values and beliefs?
- How does my understanding of the experience of developing through childhood impact upon my practice?
- How is childhood experienced in contemporary society?
- How do different social and cultural expectations influence life course development during the early childhood years?

Preparatory reading

Before you read the extract, read:

- James, A and James, A L (2004) *Constructing childhood: Theory, policy and social practice*. Basingstoke: Palgrave Macmillan. Chapter 1 'Constructing Children, Childhood and the Child'. This chapter provides an easily understood, contemporary analysis of how the concept of childhood is experienced and understood.

Extract

Morss, J R (2002) The several social constructions of James, Jenks and Prout: A contribution to the sociological theorization of childhood *The International Journal of Children's Rights 10*: pp39–54 (extracts from pp39–40 and pp51–2)

Introduction

This article is intended to contribute to the ongoing debate over theorisations of childhood, especially in the terms articulated by Allison James, Chris Jenks and Alan Prout. It focuses on the notion of "social construction" as a theory of childhood. James, Jenks and Prout (e.g. 1998) have over a number of years carefully and systematically explored alternative formulations on childhood, from the point of view of contemporary sociology (also see Hockey and James, 1993; James, 1993; James and Prout, 1997; Jenks, 1996; Prout, 2000). In describing and exploring a paradigm for the "new sociology of childhood", they have recently set out a number of possible positions that a theory of childhood might occupy. One of these is "the socially constructed child".

In the second chapter of *Theorizing Childhood* (James *et al.*, 1998) four valid approaches are defined. All four are defined as legitimately sociological in the sense of going beyond both naturalistic approaches (typical of orthodox psychology) and socialisation approaches (typical of earlier sociology). (These earlier approaches remain of contemporary relevance since they persist as available discourses, e.g. in the media or education.) The four valid approaches are: "tribal"; "social structural"; "minority group"; and "socially constructed". However, "social construction" is also a term the authors apply to their paradigm as a whole, that is, in some sense to all four of the approaches listed.

In brief, the "tribal" approach treats childhood as a kind of exotic tribe with its own beliefs, practices and institutions (employing orthodox anthropological investigations into "children's play", "children's games" and so on). The "social structural" approach treats childhood as a structurally necessary stratum in any society. The "minority group" approach treats childhood as an oppressed minority group, able to some extent (somewhat as in a parallel with the women's movement) to represent themselves and exert quasi-political action. (It is this issue of agency that distinguishes the minority group approach from the social-structural approach.) The "social construction" approach is discussed in detail below.

The authors' formulation of four approaches is an heuristic and a tentative one, but one that is rigorous enough for a number of important questions and challenges to emerge. Questions and challenges certainly arise (both explicitly and implicitly) for the notion of "social construction" in relation to childhood.

Extract from concluding remarks

Social constructionism might turn out to be almost as complex as the phenomena it seeks to portray, a genuine if a mixed blessing. There certainly seems good reason to recommend that authors should specify their own usage of the term "social construction" as precisely as possible, if they wish it to have explanatory weight.

The class of social constructionisms of childhood might turn out to be defined by the rejection of naturalistic explanation. As we have seen, this rejection is a jumping-off point for James and her colleagues. Yet there remains a lingering commitment to some kind of naturalism, in the sense of "biological immaturity" (James *et al.*, 1997: 8); thus, "childhood is not *solely* to be understood as the condition of biological immaturity" (James, 1993: 67), and children's age has to be regarded as "a cultural, *as well as* a cognitive or developmental, variable" (p. 21; all emphases added). James also notes however that an overemphasis on "social and biological immaturity" leads to the dominance of a socialisation perspective (James, 1993: 81) and her rich anthropological text includes accounts of how children manage being-a-child alongside becoming-an-adult (p. 99) and of other situations of conflicting agendas and discourses such as play-smoking (p. 172). Learning from such examples we would bracket out the child's "childness" in describing their societal locus. To put it more simply, we would be starting to treat children as humans (or "at least" as women: see Oakley, 1994).

The proposal to treat children as humans may not be as banal as it may seem; it seems to imply that there are no children's rights as such and therefore raises challenging questions concerning the United Nations Convention on the Rights of the Child, not to mention enormously problematic questions about sexuality and so on (Stainton Rogers and Stainton Rogers, 1992). Berry Mayall's discussion of her question "Are children different?" (Mayall, 1994: 116) suggests that children are different in different settings (e.g. school/home) just as adults are different in different settings (e.g. as schoolteacher, parent), and implies quite radically, that *children are no different from adults* except as the consequence of treatment and of their own (interlinked) activity. That is to say, children are people who are treated, by themselves and/or by others, *as* "children". And of course as Mayall observes, these proposals "fly in the face of the essential propositions of developmentalism" (see Morss, 1996). Hood-Williams' words of a decade ago surely remain as true now, and as present to us in their urgency as well as in their compassion:

> [W]e need to begin with a conception of patriarchal authority that even today maintains childhood as a firmly exclusionary status; we need to take serious account of the cross cuttings between age and gender; we need an agenda that is much more sensitive to questions of power and control; we need to recognize children as active, if excluded, subjects and not as the incompetent objects of adult policies; we need to see children as [sic] social relationships in which our very understanding of childhood is constructed out of our notions of adulthood. In all of this we have hardly begun. (Hood-Williams, 1990: 170–171)

Analysis

The extract above is taken from the introduction and concluding remarks of a journal article. It is intended that you will find reading this extract, and the whole article if you have time, to be useful on two levels. Firstly, Morss' article is a critique of the approach and theoretical stance of a set of authors, James, A, Jenks, C and Prout, A (the first of these authors is also the co-author of the pre-reading text suggested above). In his article, Morss challenges, questions and scrutinises their approach. I would suggest that Morss' analysis is robust, as he presents a coherent argument with logical debate, which is supported by source materials. Therefore, although you may find the extract to be written in a complex linguistic style, the underlying principals of academic writing that Morss has adhered to, provide a useful example of how to take a critical, evaluative stance in your own approach to theories, texts and research. As you read the extract above, which was written in 2002, you should critique Morss' approach, deconstructing his ideas and analysing whether his stance is relevant and applicable to understanding childhood in Britain today. Secondly, the content of the extract offers a critique on how the concept of childhood is explained, understood and given meaning in our society. This is considered further in the discussion below.

You may feel that devoting this section of the chapter to understanding the concept of childhood is unnecessary. After all, it is fair to assume that we have all been children and so may think that we all understand what childhood is. However, whilst we have memories and our individual experiences of childhood may have been influential in our life course development, Mayall (2000) reminds us that only children know what it is like to be a child. Indeed, with respect to our interpretation of this phase of life, the article and the pre-reading have shown that this is not as straightforward as it may seem.

Once childhood was a feature of parental (maybe just maternal) discourse, the currency of educators and the sole theoretical property of developmental psychology. Now with an intensity perhaps unprecedented, childhood has become popularised, politicised, scrutinised and analysed in a series of interlocking spaces in which the traditional and certainty about childhood and children's social status are being radically undermined.

(James et al., 1998, page 3)

The social constructionist approach, being critiqued by Morss in his article, develops an understanding of childhood that is dependent upon the person's broader ideological perceptions of the world. This means that the concept of childhood cannot be scientifically, objectively or factually explained. Its definition cannot be taken for granted, but rather, understanding childhood requires interpretation and meanings to be imposed. Thus, your views or perspectives on what childhood is, are informed or underpinned by your experiences, assumptions, culture, values, beliefs, situation and circumstances. The logical consequence of this approach is that the differences in behaviours and attitudes towards children reflect historical, cultural and social beliefs about childhood, and different ideas and expectations about how children develop. These differences, in turn, may be seen as leading to cultural and historical divergence in children's social and economic roles and the developmental trajectories that children experience.

In his concluding remarks, Morss draws out some of the complexities of social constructionism and, using the example of *play-smoking* (pretending to smoke), discusses the perceived conflicts of childhood. You may be able to think of other similar examples, indeed the notion of *being-a-child alongside becoming-an-adult* and the contradictory messages that are portrayed through society could be argued to be apparent in national policy and strategy, one example being in the proposed Child Care Bill, introduced into parliament in November 2005 (www.dfes.gov.uk). This Bill provides a framework for services providing education and care to children under five years of age. As you read this text, the Child Care Bill may be at a different stage in the parliamentary process. Nevertheless, it is interesting to consider which of the social constructions described in the extract, might be inherent in this policy: *tribal*; *social structural*; *minority group*; or *social construction*? You may feel that childhood is being interpreted in yet a different way by the policy makers.

Morss moves on to cite the work of Mayall and the contentious view that children are only children because of the way that they are treated. This hypothesis has strong links to social constructionism, for Mayall acknowledges that children develop biologically and physically, but adds that development is also influenced by social, historical and political factors. In the final quotation of the extract, some thought-provoking challenges are set out, and again you could consider these ideas and whether in current policies, such as *Every child matters* and the Child Care Bill, children are being recognised as *active, if excluded, subjects and not as the incompetent objects of adult policies.*

There are no direct answers to these issues. They are matters for analysis and discussion but, as you reflect upon them you will begin to develop a deeper understanding of how you perceive the concept of childhood and your own values and beliefs. It might also give you some indication of how childhood is experienced in contemporary society.

In summary, the extract is from an article that deconstructs the *social construction of childhood*. Morss does not disagree that childhood is socially constructed, but discusses this approach further, drawing out the underlying assumptions and adding to the debate. From this perspective, the experience of, and development during, childhood is seen as being socially and culturally defined. Images of childhood, attitudes, beliefs and expectations about children become seen as factual, self-evident and obvious, whereas in fact they are *the products of human meaning-making* (Woodhead and Montgomery, 2003, page 26).

As you progress further through this book you will identify themes that can be seen to be relevant across the whole of the life course, for example change and continuity, and similarity and difference. This section and the following sections that explore physical, mental and emotional development, followed by security and safety in childhood, further develop these themes through an exploration of how children grow, learn, change and develop through this early stage of the life course.

Personal reflections

As stated in the analysis above, we have all been children and so might feel that we all understand what childhood is. You will have feelings, thoughts and memories about your childhood experiences and the part those experiences had to play in influencing your life course and development to date. You may be a parent, or have other close relationships with children and you may have strong beliefs and ideas about children and how they should be perceived.

Reflect upon your own values and beliefs in respect of children and childhood and your reading of the extract and analysis above. Then write down short responses to the questions below.

• How has your perception and understanding of childhood developed? Make a list of the different aspects of your life course that have influenced your thoughts and construction of childhood.
• What are the practical consequences of the way in which you make sense of childhood, in terms of your response to children and your expectations of them?

Comment

It is likely that your values and beliefs about childhood have been shaped by many different influences across your life course so far. These may have included your parents, the media, your peers, the community in which you grew up, culture, your age now and the period you grew up in, your experience of being with, working with or having children and so on! Given the many facets that influence the meanings we construct, you may also appreciate that these meanings can change and evolve as we, and the society around us, change and develop. You may also realise, from your reflections, how difficult it is to envisage a society where the concept of *child* or *childhood* has not been given meaning and therefore does not exist.

Thus, the practical consequences of the way in which we make sense of childhood follow from the assumptions that underpin our constructions. So, for example, your beliefs about how children should behave, what is right and wrong, what should be expected of children at particular ages, even what children should wear or look like, will be influenced by your values and beliefs.

Practical implications and activities

In the earlier analysis, it was suggested that you consider the way in which a particular piece of developing legislation, the Child Care Bill, constructs the notion of children and childhood.

Having now reflected upon your own assumptions, values and beliefs in respect of children and childhood, you can examine the ways in which childhood is interpreted by policy makers and whether those interpretations mirror your own assumptions and expectations. Furthermore, and significantly for the purposes of this chapter and this book, you can begin to evaluate the implications of how childhood is defined in policy, law and strategy for direct social work practice with children.

Physical, mental and emotional development in early childhood

The previous section of this chapter demonstrated how national policy and legislation is one of many influences on our understanding and expectations of development through childhood. In this part of the chapter you will focus on particular aspects of early childhood development: physical, mental and emotional development, as encompassed within two of the stated aims of *Every child matters* (DfES, 2004), within the strategic outcome, *be healthy*.

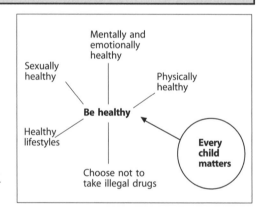

Figure 2.2.
Adapted from *Every child matters: Change for children* (DfES, 2004)

It is not possible to explore every facet of physical, mental and emotional development in early childhood within the scope of this section. Therefore, as with other sections of this book, the pre-reading, extracts, analysis and activities are provided as signposts to stimulate reflection and direct your further study. The reflective questions that you should contemplate as you study this section are:

- how do different perspectives and theories explain physical and emotional development in early childhood?
- how is physical and emotional development in early childhood understood and assessed?
- in what ways does knowledge of physical and emotional development in early childhood inform social work practice?

Preparatory reading

Before you read the extract, read:

- Department for Education and Skills (DfES) (2004) *Every child matters*, Cm 5860. London: Stationery Office. **www.dfes.gov.uk**
  For this section it would be helpful if you familiarise yourself with Chapter 2 'Strong foundations', pages 25–36 and Chapter 3 'Supporting parents and carers', pages 39–49.
- Department for Education and Skills (DfES) (2002) *Birth to three matters: A framework to support children in their earliest years.* **www.surestart.gov.uk**
  This is a framework, developed to support practitioners working with young children. It was developed using research findings and practitioner perspectives and includes four aspects. One of the four aspects is entitled *A healthy child* – see page 7 of the document – and incorporates physical and emotional development.
- Department of Health (DoH) (2004) *National service framework for children, young people and maternity services.* London: Stationery Office.
  Standard 1: 'Promoting health and well-being, identifying needs and intervening early' is particularly relevant to this part of Chapter 2.

These documents provide an indication of the contemporary strategic, structural and planning context in which young children develop physically, mentally and emotionally in Britain today. The following extract aims to stimulate your thoughts and ideas about the ways in which physical and biological development in early childhood is understood. This is followed by a second extract, which focuses on emotional development during early childhood. The analysis section then encourages discussion and debate about both extracts and the related preparatory reading above.

Extract

James, A and James, A L (2004) *Constructing childhood: Theory, policy and social practice.* **Basingstoke: Palgrave Macmillan, Chapter 2, pp142–6, 'Childhood: a process of natural growth and development'.**

Childhood: a process of natural growth and development

Naturalistic and scientific approaches to health and the body hold that 'the capabilities and constraints of human bodies define individuals' and that the health differences and resultant inequalities, which are to be found in the social world, are simply manifestations of the 'determining power of the biological body' (Shilling 1993: 41). Thus, for example, sexual difference is a taken-for-granted feature of bodies and held to account for the 'natural' propensity of women for mothering and of men for dominance, bodily differences that in turn are often used to provide justification for gendered social and political inequalities. In a similar way, as noted earlier in Chapter 1, childhood is naturalised through the child's body. Commonly envisaged as the literal embodiment of change over time – the phrase 'when you grow up' makes this quite explicit – concepts of childhood have long been seen through the lens of children's bodily development and change. Children's social identities as children are understood as a 'natural' outcome of their bodily difference from adults and their trajectory of physical development prized in terms of the 'futurity' of the nation (Jenks 1996b).

However, exactly, what is 'normal' and 'standard' in terms of children's development and the extent to which normalcy can indeed be generalised and measured in this way for all children, can be questioned both in terms of the hegemony of particular scientific paradigms and with regard to the social and political consequences for children themselves of employing such measures. Historians of childhood are, for example, beginning to document the ways in which ideas of standardisation, measurement and normalcy in relation to children's physical development emerged as devices with which to monitor and regulate children. Steedman, for example, argues that it was the 19th century that,

> fixed childhood, not just as a category of experience, but also as a time span ... [through] the development of mass schooling, and its grouping of children together by age cohort. In the same period the practices of child psychology, developmental linguistics and anthropometry provided clearer pictures of what children were like, and how they should be expected to look at certain ages.
>
> (Steedman 1995: 7)

During this period, the idea of a standardised path for child growth and development was used to underpin a whole variety of social, political and educational policies, policies designed to ensure a successful outcome for the whole child – that is, the achievement of adulthood:

> The building up of scientific evidence about physical growth in childhood described an actual progress in individual lives, which increased in symbolic importance during the nineteenth century, whereby that which is traversed is, in the end, left behind and abandoned, as the child grows up and goes away. In this way, childhood as it has been culturally described is always about that which is temporary and impermanent, always describes a loss in adult life, a state that is recognised too late. Children are quite precisely a physiological chronology, a history, as they make their way through the stages of growth.
>
> (Steedman 1992: 37)

Thus, during the 19th century an understanding of the importance of child health was becoming central to the shoring up of the conceptual space of childhood for children, a space which was being carved out, simultaneously, in other areas through, for example, the institutionalisation of compulsory schooling (see Chapter 5) and the Factory Acts that removed children, progressively, from the sphere of work. Thus, as Armstrong (1995) has shown, the wide-scale surveying of the child population gradually began to define certain limits of normality for children's bodies. This was exemplified in the height and weight growth chart, which was first introduced in the early 20th century and is still used routinely today to 'check' a child's development. Measurements are made of a child's height and weight at different points in time and these are then plotted against three pre-inscribed growth lines, known as percentiles, which define the boundaries of normalcy for low, medium and high growth rates.

As Armstrong notes, the development of this chart meant that 'every child could be assigned a place on the chart and, with successive plots, given a personal trajectory' for the future, a process which, it was believed, would reveal those children most at risk.

Thus, as Steedman shows, the introduction of such devices enabled the plight of working-class children to be highlighted by the political activists and reformers of the period in their call for social change:

> [Child physiology] structured around the idea of growth and development ... allowed for comparisons to be made between children, and, most important of all as a basis for a social policy on childhood, it... rooted mental life in the material body and the material conditions of life. In this way, working-class children could be seen as having been robbed of natural development, their potential for health and growth lying dormant in their half-starved bodies.
>
> (Steedman 1992: 25)

Such a review of children and childhood – the explicit linking of children's health to the future welfare of the nation – was a consistent feature of 19th century social and political thought. This in itself bears witness to the gradual ideological shoring up of childhood as a particular social space via social policy, through the notion that children have special and very particular physical and mental health care needs different from those of adults. Thus it was that paediatrics developed as a specialist branch of medicine in the early 20th century and, as the surveying and monitoring of the child population proceeded, other specialist children's clinics and services followed close behind. This was, Armstrong (1983) notes, accompanied by a shift from seeing 'pathology' as not just located within the body of the child but also in its environment – in poverty, poor education, bad parenting and dysfunctional families (see Chapter 8).

However, as Armstrong observes, although the height and weight chart claims to depict a child's unique and individual development, this uniqueness only exists in the context of a 'generalised' child, derived epidemiologically from the population as a whole. Against this, the 'normality' or 'abnormality' of each individual child is measured and in this, 'age' – that is, time passing – is critical, for it provides the context within which 'successful' or 'pathological' height/weight trajectories are charted. Thus, the health of the child's body, he argues, is 'delineated not by the absolute categories of physiology and pathology, but by the characteristics of the normal population', shared and common characteristics that become standardised as 'normality' (1995: 397).

In this way, 'normality' for children has become firmly linked to the trajectory of a *collective* model of age-based change and development, inscribed upon and through the *individual* body (and mind) of 'the child'. And one consequence of this charting of 'normalcy' is that any child is always potentially at risk of 'precocity' – doing things earlier than s/he *should* – or its opposite, developmental delay – doing things later than s/he *should*. Thus although, as Freeman (1992) notes, within any population individual deviations from the norms for the group are bound to be found, through the intense surveillance of children's growth and development the fear is that 'difference' becomes pathologised as 'deviance'.

Therefore, as Freeman also observes, what such statistically based surveillance techniques do is to open up 'an epistemological space in which the politics of social intervention ... are played out' (1992: 36). Who gets what kind of intervention, why and when become, then, highly politicised issues of citizenship and of rights.

Extract

Woodhead, M and Montgomery, H (2003) *Understanding Childhood: an interdisciplinary approach* **Chichester: Wiley and Sons Ltd (pp103–6) Section 2.3 Natural Needs?**

Babies and young children often get upset if they are separated from their parents, or from the people who most often care for them. What's less well known is that babies' tendency to get upset follows a developmental pattern. *Separation protest* (as psychologists call this kind of crying) begins to happen more often when babies are around seven to eight months of age. Younger babies are less sensitive to being separated – or at least they don't protest so loudly. *Separation protest* typically reaches a peak around twelve months and then gradually becomes less frequent as most babies become better able to cope with brief separation. Cross-cultural research has also found the same developmental patterns in very varying cultural contexts (see Figure 1). These are generalizations of course, and there can be marked individual as well as cultural differences in the ways separations are managed. Also, a change of care arrangements (such as starting nursery) can cause renewed upset in much older children.

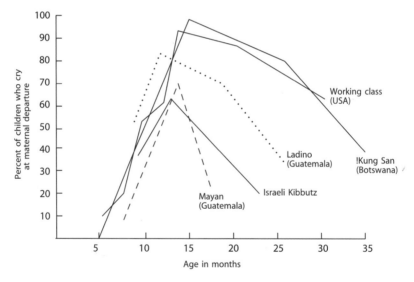

Figure 1 Separation protest shown by babies from five different groups around the world. Source: Adapted from Kagan, 1876, pp 186–96.

You may recall that Darwin included the development of affection in his study of his son Doddy, noting that Doddy was several months old before he seemed to show a clear preference for his nurse's affections. The onset of separation protest during the second half of the first year is now recognized as an indicator that the young child has formed emotional *attachments* to a parent or other care-giver. This line of research originated with studies carried out by Bowlby in the 1930s, exploring the effects on children of being deprived of maternal care. Bowlby wanted to explain why children brought up in baby homes, orphanages and other institutions common in England at that time so often had relationship difficulties and behavioural problems later on. He was also concerned about the emotional distress experienced by young children in hospital who were deprived of contact with their parents (also common practice in England at the time). Notice the parallels between Bowlby's interest in the effects of social deprivation, and Itard's interest in the deprivations suffered by the Wild Boy of Aveyron.

Bowlby's background was in medicine and he was trained in psychoanalysis. He was also very interested in the study of evolution, especially the lessons from ethological research into animal behaviour. Ethological studies of baby geese seemed to show that young goslings imprint on their mother (or indeed the first moving thing with which they come into contact) (Lorenz, 1981). Bowlby saw a strong parallel in the way young babies become attached (or bonded) to their mothers (or other principal carers). He argued that a baby becomes distressed and resists separation because of a biologically adaptive mechanism which evolved to protect the young of the human species by ensuring an infant remains in close proximity to their mother.

One of the most controversial features of Bowlby's early theories is that he took the bold step of trying to prescribe children's needs for care. In a famous report to the World Health Organization he argued that some ways of caring for babies are natural and healthy; others are unnatural and harmful. Bowlby's often-quoted conclusion at this time was:

> [W]hat is believed to be essential for mental health is that an infant and young child should experience a warm, intimate, and continuous relationship with his mother (or permanent mother-substitute – one person who steadily 'mothers' him in which both find satisfaction and enjoyment.
>
> (Bowlby, 1953, p. 13)

Bowlby's work had a major impact on reforming practices in child care, especially in residential and hospital care. At the same time these early theories were criticized on two counts, which centre on the claim that children's emotional needs are an expression of their human nature.

The first set of criticisms drew attention to the dangers of over-generalizing from behaviours of other species. Observations of animal imprinting were translated into theories about mother–infant bonding. The problem is that human infants don't 'bond' with their care-givers in a mechanical or instinctive way equivalent to imprinting. A baby's first relationships are also built on communication, and the beginnings of shared understanding.

The second set of criticisms centred on claims made for 'natural' care. Critics argued that these so-called natural patterns of care were a reflection of Western cultural values, projected onto children as being about their needs. They were seen as a social construction, reinforcing dominant attitudes to family life in post-war Britain, by emphasizing women's responsibilities for meeting the needs of their infants through offering full-time mothering (Tizard, 1991). For example, Bowlby's original work argued that children's needs for love and security are focused on one person (the mother or mother substitute). This principle (known as *monotropism*) was widely criticized for telling as much about mid-twentieth century English attitudes to family, nursery care and gender divisions as about the fundamental needs of children. It contradicted a wide range of evidence from cultural contexts where shared care is the norm, for example, the widespread practice of older siblings (usually older sisters) sharing care of young children (Weisner and Gallimore, 1977).

To summarize, firstly, children have needs for care and nurture, but their attachments aren't necessarily focused on one person and they may be distributed amongst several consistent care-givers. Secondly, developmental theories may be informed by careful empirical research, but the interpretation of that research is shaped by available discourses about children's needs for care and nurture.

Analysis

Both extracts are taken from academic texts and both, therefore, present the views of their respective authors. The first extract discusses some of the assumptions and issues that James and James (2004) associate with approaches to understanding physical or biological development in children. The second extract critiques some of the ideas about early emotional development, in particular attachment theories. As you read the extracts, you may agree with, or wish to challenge some aspects of the arguments put forward.

James and James (2004) challenge standardised measurements of physical development in childhood, questioning how development can be generalised or defined as *normal* or *universally expected* in this way. Similarly the critique developed by Woodhead and Montgomery (2003) in part, questions generalisations that they perceive in Bowlby's attachment theory. The issue of how far childhood development can be predicted, or explained as following a predetermined path, raises the well-rehearsed *nature versus nurture* debate. (If you are unfamiliar with the fundamental assumptions on each side of this debate, Crawford and Walker (2003, page 10) provide a useful summary.) James and James (2004) go on to suggest that, on the one hand, charting and measuring physical development provides a fundamental way of identifying the impact of social policy on child development. However, on the other hand, such categorising of children's progress leads to certain definitions of what is normal, with development that falls outside of that being seen as problematic. An example of this biological approach is the influential work of Mary Sheridan who advocates that professionals working with children *should be familiar with the accepted milestones* so that they can recognise *the earliest signs of deviation from normal development* (Sheridan, 1975, page 1). Sheridan provides a guide to children's physical developmental progress from birth to five years, with charts for clinical testing, which reflect *four human biological achievements*: posture and movement; vision and fine movements; hearing and speech; and social behaviour and play. You may notice that similar categories are utilised in the *Birth to three matters* framework that you were guided to, as part of the pre-reading for this section. Within this framework (page 14), four broad areas of development are suggested, although it is acknowledged that *growth and development are less predictable for some children than for others.*

There is, therefore, a debate about how physical and biological growth and development in childhood is understood, assessed, measured and perceived. This debate is very important for social work practitioners to evaluate in respect of their role in assessment and intervention in children's lives. The Common Assessment Framework (CAF), which is an integral element of the strategic direction outlined in *Every child matters*, incorporates three domains:

- how well a child is developing, including in their health and progress in learning;
- how well parents or carers are able to support their child's development and respond appropriately to any needs;
- the impact of wider family and environmental elements on the child's development and on the capacity of their parents and carers.

DfES (2006, page 17)

These key themes are then each broken down and given in more detail, as shown in the table below.

Domains	Elements
Development of child	• Health – general health, physical development and speech. • Emotional and social development. • Behavioural development. • Identity, including self-esteem, self-image and social presentation. • Family and social relationships. • Self-care skills and independence. • Learning – Understanding, reasoning and problem solving, participation in learning, education and employment, progress and achievement in learning, aspirations.
Parents and carers	• Basic care, ensuring safety and protection. • Emotional warmth and stability. • Guidance, boundaries and stimulation.
Family and enviromental	• Family history, functioning and well-being. • Wider family. • Housing, employment and financial considerations. • Social and community elements and resources, including education.

Figure 2.3 Common Assessment Framework: Assessment elements and domains

Department for Education and Skills (DfES) (2006, Annex A) *Framework for children and young people: Guide for service managers and practitioners.* **www.dfes.gov.uk**

The CAF is built on the principles of integrated services, multi-agency working and shared information. As such, it is difficult to envisage how practitioners from different disciplines and agencies across health, social care and education, will be able to effectively implement this policy without coherent, agreed, underlying frameworks, measures or models against which to begin to formulate their identification, professional judgement and understanding of children's needs. However, the CAF does not have to be undertaken ridgidly (DfES, 2006, page 13); it is a means of collating information, including the views of children and carers, upon which to base professional judgement about the holistic needs of the child. It is those professional judgements that should be explicitly constructed and informed by evidence from research, theory and an established knowledge-base.

From the table above you can distinguish those areas of the CAF that are explicitly related to physical development. It is also possible to identify, as it is a particular element within the framework, *emotional and social development*. However, it could be argued that many of the elements, across all three of the domains, relate to areas of a child's life course that may influence their emotional growth. In the second extract, Woodhead and Montgomery (2003) discuss emotional development as explained by attachment theories; hence there is a clear association with the CAF domains relating to *parents and carers* and *family and environmental*.

Emotions and emotional development are complex concepts related to individual feelings, thoughts and self-esteem and the impact that they have upon behaviour. In the *Birth to three matters* (DfES, 2002) framework, *emotional well-being* is described as including:

> relationships, which are close, warm and supportive; being able to express feelings such as joy, sadness, frustration and fear, leading to the development of strategies to cope with new, challenging or stressful situations.

> Emotional stability and resilience including
> – Being special to someone
> – Being able to express feelings
> – Developing healthy dependence
> – Developing healthy independence

(DfES, 2002 pages 7 and 11)

Woodhead and Montgomery's (2003) main premise is that whilst attachment and care are significant influences on early childhood development, the form of that attachment need not be prescriptive and examples of cultural or historical variation in child care demonstrate a need to take a broader perspective on the ways in which children develop emotionally. In respect of social work practice, Williams (2005, page 150) supports this view, stating that attachment theory has developed to incorporate a wider understanding of different relationships and, as such, it underpins social work practice with children, particularly those in residential care or for whom the plan is adoption. Williams (ibid) states that attachment issues should be addressed within the care planning process, which we have seen is underpinned by the information gathered through the assessment. The significance of attachment theory to the assessment of children in need is also raised within practice guidance issued by the National Assembly for Wales: *The wealth of research on attachment reinforces the importance of paying attention to attachment in assessments of all children, irrespective of their age* (DoH, 2001, page 5). If you are interested in exploring the issue of children's emotional and behavioural development further, and looking at how this may be assessed as part of social work practice within a multi-disciplinary assessment, Jowitt and O'Loughlin (2005, page 60) provide a helpful overview of the areas that would be taken into account.

Personal reflections

In this section of the chapter you have focused on examining certain perspectives on physical and emotional development in early childhood. Your reading has been set in context through explicit links to national policy and legislation, in particular through the outcome *be healthy,* which is one of the five key outcomes of *Every child matters* (DfES, 2004).

You should now take the opportunity to think about what you perceive as the main determinants of a *'healthy child'.*

- Write down the key words that come to your mind as you try to describe a child who you would consider physically and emotionally *healthy.*

- Then look back over your list and, for each response, think about how you would assess or 'measure' each individual child against that criterion.

Finally, reviewing your work from the above activity, can you summarise your own perspective on physical and emotional development in early childhood? Also, how does your thinking and your learning from this section of the chapter inform and influence your social work practice with young children?

Comment

You may have approached the above activity very systematically, drawing explicitly on your learning from this section, or you may have come up with a quick list of ideas that have less structure, but are nonetheless comprehensive. The CAF domains and elements shown in the table earlier in the chapter, offer one possible starting point for this activity. Another option would be to use the *Birth to three matters* framework (suggested as pre-reading for this section), which offers four aspects: a strong child; a skilful communicator; a competent learner; and a healthy child. This fourth aspect, a healthy child, would be particularly relevant here. The *Birth to three matters* framework suggests a healthy child demonstrates the following:

A healthy child	
Emotional well-being – Emotional stability and resilience	• Being special to someone • Being able to express feelings • Developing healthy dependence • Developing healthy independence
Growing and developing – Physical well-being	• Being well nourished • Being active, rested and protected • Gaining control of the body • Acquiring physical skills
Keeping safe – Being safe and protected	• Discovering boundaries and limits • Learning about rules • Knowing when and how to ask for help • Learning when to say no and anticipating when others will do so
Healthy choices – Being able to make choices	• Discovering and learning about his/her body • Demonstrating individual preferences • Making decisions • Becoming aware of others and their needs

Department for Education and Skills (DfES) (2002) *Birth to three matters: A framework to support children in their earliest years.* **www.surestart.gov.uk**

Figure 2.4 Birth to three matters – a healthy child

Adapted from Every child matters: Change for children (DfES, 2004)

The second part of the activity, however, is more problematic. You have seen how very specific scales and measures exist to assess milestones in physical development, but that these have to be implemented with caution. In assessing emotional development, however, shared professional judgement, alongside the views and experiences expressed by the child and parent/carer, may be the main process for assessment decisions.

Practical implications and activities

As you have seen earlier in this section, the common assessment is a mechanism for drawing together a range of information about a child's development and the support available to them. Imagine that you had been asked to draw up a list of ten statements of good practice which aim to ensure that assessments are effective and accurate. Write out your ten statements, and then refer to *The Common Assessment Framework for children and young people: Practitioners' Guide* (DfES, 2006) particularly pages 13–21 which offer practice guidance on the completion of the common assessment.

The significance of safety, security and stability for childhood development

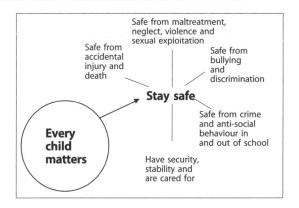

Figure 2.5 Stay safe
Adapted from Every child matters: Change for children (DfES, 2004)

Chapter 4 of *Every Child Matters* (DfES 2004) is entitled 'Early intervention and effective protection'. Within the chapter, drawing upon The Victoria Climbié Inquiry (Laming, 2003), the significance of joint working across professional and agency boundaries is stressed. Similarly the *National Service Framework (NSF) for children, young people and maternity services* (DoH, 2004) states, within Standard 5, that *safeguarding and promoting the welfare of children is prioritised by all agencies, working in partnership to plan and provide co-ordinated and comprehensive services in line with national guidance and legislation.*

This final section of Chapter 2, considers the *Every child matters* (DfES, 2004) strategic outcome, *stay safe*. In particular, you will be encouraged to reflect upon the possible impact of abuse and neglect on children's development. Whilst this chapter has focused on the early years of childhood, the extract provided considers research into the relationship between maltreatment and a range of problems children may experience at school. Therefore, this section of the chapter actually relates to developmental issues across the whole of childhood and provides the 'bridge' to your reading in the next chapter. It also draws together your learning from the earlier parts of this chapter, in that

> The sustained abuse or neglect of children physically, emotionally or sexually can have major long-term effects on all aspects of a child's health, development and well-being. (DoH, 1999, page 6)

Thus, the reflective prompts suggested earlier in the chapter are also relevant as you read the pre-reading, extract and analysis to follow. Additionally, the questions that you should think about as you read through this section of the chapter are:

- what does this tell me about my social work practice?
- what does this tell me about professional social work more broadly?
- in what ways might issues of safety, security and stability impact on child development?

Preparatory reading

Before you read this extract, read:

- Department for Education and Skills (DfES) (2004) *Every child matters*, Cm 5860 London: Stationery Office. **www.dfes.gov.uk**
  For this section it would be helpful if you familiarise yourself with Chapter 4.
- Department of Health (DoH) (2004) *National Service Framework for children, young people and maternity services.* London: Stationery Office.
  Standard 5 is particularly relevant to this part of Chapter 2.
- Department of Health (DoH) (1999) *Working together to safeguard children.* London: The Stationery Office.
  This document sets out the policy and procedures for all agencies and professionals working together to promote children's welfare and to protect children from abuse and neglect. Whilst the whole document is relevant to your studies about child development, for this section, pages 6 and 7, which outline the 'Impact of abuse and neglect' are particularly relevant.

Extract

Mills, C (2004*) Problems at home, problems at school: The effects of maltreatment in the home on children's functioning at school: an overview of recent research.* **London: NSPCC Introduction, pages 10–12.**

Children's functioning at school

In this review, when we refer to children's functioning at school, we are encompassing the wide range of behaviours and activities which children are expected to engage in at school. As with the concept of child maltreatment, how children should behave at school and what they are expected to achieve are not absolutes that are static across time. The expectations of children at the beginning of the twenty-first century are radically different to those which existed at the beginning of the twentieth century. Nevertheless, it is possible to state with some precision what current expectations are of how children should function at school. These expectations can be summarised as follows:

- to attend, unless too ill to do so
- to behave respectfully to school staff and peers
- to work hard and achieve the best academic results possible
- to learn and develop
- to benefit from the school experience both intellectually and socially.

Child maltreatment and children's functioning at school

In a recent systematic review of the literature, Veltman and Brown[29] identified 92 studies conducted between 1967 and 2000 which examined the relationship between child maltreatment and cognitive development, intelligence, language and school achievement. The majority had been conducted in the USA, although a small number of studies were conducted in Canada, Britain and Australia. They found that:

- 31 out of 34 studies (91 per cent) showed that maltreatment was related to poor school achievement
- delays in cognitive development were shown in 49 out of 65 studies (75 per cent)
- delays in language development were shown in 36 out of 42 studies (86 per cent).

In our survey of the literature we have also found evidence that maltreated children are:

- at greater risk of poor school behaviour
- at greater risk of being the victims of bullying in school
- more likely to have special educational needs
- at greater risk of exclusion from school
- more likely to be absent from school.

Thus the literature shows a clear relationship between maltreatment and children's functioning at school.

Cause and effect

Veltman and Browne are critical of the methods used in a minority of the studies that they reviewed. A significant weakness of some of the earlier research was that it did not use a group of children who had not been maltreated as a control. The problem with this is that simply looking at the academic achievement of a group of maltreated children (and finding it well below average) does not establish that maltreatment is linked to poor school achievement. Poor school performance may be the result of some other factor which maltreated children share in common with non-maltreated children who also do badly at school. For example, it is known that a child's socio-economic status is strongly related to educational outcomes.[30] Children from deprived families generally do not do as well at school as those from wealthy homes.

Social scientists have adopted a number of techniques to control for factors like socio-economic status (sometimes referred to as "confounder variables"). One approach is to ensure that the performance of a group of maltreated children is compared with that of a group of non-maltreated children, who are "matched" for socio-economic status. In other words children in both groups have comparable home circumstances, except for the presence or absence of abuse.

In practice it has been found necessary to try to match children on a range of factors in addition to their socio-economic status, for example age, gender, ethnic origin, neighbourhood of residence and birth order.

Even when it is found that maltreated children are more likely to do poorly at school than a matched control group, this still does not establish that maltreatment is the cause of poor school performance. There may be some additional unknown factor which is the cause of both. Veltman and Browne suggest that one way of addressing this difficulty would be to measure the children's intellectual abilities both before they have been maltreated and after they have been maltreated. This would show that maltreatment was the crucial factor. However, in practice this is it not possible. The nature of child maltreatment is such that it is often difficult to know exactly and reliably when abuse first occurs.

Other approaches are ruled out for ethical reasons. Researchers cannot experiment with children's lives in order to see if maltreatment is the key factor which affects their performance at school (for example, by protecting one group of children from abuse but not another).

It is difficult not to conclude that social research has its limitations. It is often restricted to exploring correlations rather than causes. Neither this study nor other reviews have discovered research which shows conclusively that child maltreatment is a cause of children's poor functioning at school. Indeed such research may be an unachievable gold standard.

However, the majority of the studies reported here have taken meticulous care to isolate child maltreatment and to look at its relationship to children's functioning at school independently of other variables which may also be causal factors. Researchers are also able to call on advanced statistical techniques to compensate for the effects of "confounder variables" in the analysis of the data.

The conclusion that can be drawn is that child maltreatment and children's poor functioning at school are closely connected phenomena and that this is not accounted for by any obvious third factor, such as socio-economic status. This implies that researchers and practitioners need to give close attention to the educational needs of maltreated children. It also implies that where children are experiencing difficulties at school, teachers should be particularly alert for other signs which may indicate that these difficulties are associated with maltreatment in the home.

[29] Veltman, M. and Browne, K. (2001) "Three decades of child maltreatment research: implications for the school years", *Trauma, Violence and Abuse*, Vol. 9, No. 3, pp. 915–39.

[30] Feinstein, L. (9003) "Inequality in the early cognitive development of British children in the 1970 cohort", *Economica*, Vol. 70, pp. 73–97.

Analysis

This extract is taken from an extensive review of research that examines the relationship between how children are treated at home and how they progress at school. The review was undertaken following publication of the green paper *Every child matters* and looks at how abuse and neglect may impact upon *academic performance, special educational needs, behaviour problems, bullying, absence and exclusion* and *psychiatric conditions.*

As with earlier extracts, this extract provides a critique of research methodologies, which is, in itself, another useful example of evaluation and critical, analytical writing style. However, more significantly for this section of the chapter, Mills (2004, page 11) concludes that there is a clear link between child abuse and problems in school. You may feel that this is somewhat unremarkable and something that is to be expected. Yet, as Mills notes in his opening paragraph to this review document, it is only very recently that national strategies are moving towards the integration of educational and social care services for children. Furthermore, Mills' critique in this chapter can help you to understand that this 'taken-for-granted' approach actually simplifies the premise of cause and effect. So, for example, a whole range of other variables, or inconsistencies and differences, between children might explain or influence the correlation between abuse/neglect and developmental difference. In the extract, Mills cites the influence of a child's socio-economic status on educational outcomes. Similarly *Messages from research* (DoH, 1995) drew out the relationship between poverty and child abuse and neglect. Additionally, as shown throughout this book, there are many other factors which influence development and any, or all of these could have some bearing on this cause:effect equation, for example: the child's age and gender; ethnic origin, culture;

their experience of family life. Additionally, Mills' final statement in this extract appears to be very specific in making the association with issues *in the home*. His definition of *home* is not made clear here and it is possible that he is referring to the child's wider out-of-school experiences. However, his perspective could be seen to be taking a very narrow approach to children's lives. Children in contemporary society are likely to have a wide and complex range of experiences, networks and environments that influence their growth and development. Therefore reference to only 'home' and 'school' could be seen to prohibit the adoption of a holistic approach.

> Children's lives outside the home usually become increasingly important, they have friends, join clubs, are involved in sports and so on ... Because of the number of changes to which the child is subject adversity or abuse can have further dramatic effects on the child's life. (Daniel et al., 1999, page 197)

A holistic approach to identifying and responding to the needs of a child, particularly where there are concerns about issues of safety, requires knowledge and understanding of child growth and development (Crawford and Walker, 2003, page 50). There are many potential ways in which exposure to risk and danger, including abuse, neglect or maltreatment, may influence a child's development. In the first section of the extract, Mills provides some empirical, statistical data to support his work, but within this mentions cognitive development, language development and intelligence. Your pre-reading for this section, particularly from the *Working together to safeguard children* (DoH, 1999) document, will have alerted you to many more aspects of childhood development that may be affected by insecurity, neglect and harm, further examples being the child's self-image, self-esteem and emotional, physical and psychological development. Additionally, abuse and neglect experienced during childhood may have a longer term impact on life course development into adulthood (DoH, 1999, page 6). Rutter (cited in Daniel et al., 1999, page 229) describes *developmental pathways* and highlights the role of school experiences in determining not only cognitive development, but also self-esteem and self-efficacy, which, in turn, provide protective and resilience factors to enable children and young people to have more control over their lives.

In the extract and in this analysis there has been very little explicit discussion about social work practice. However, the research review and the policy documents suggested as pre-reading actually indicate significant implications for individual social workers and for the profession and service of social work. The following activities aim to stimulate your reflections and further study in social work practice with children, where there are concerns about safety, particularly in respect of the different aspects of their development.

Personal reflections

Following your reading of this extract, the analysis and the pre-reading materials, think about your developing social work practice with children. The area of child protection in social work is vast, so you should focus here on how, within your practice, you can identify where issues of safety, risk and harm can impact on a child's development. Make a list of key 'good practice' points that you could incorporate into your practice with children in this respect.

Comment

This activity is not necessarily straightforward as the first point would need to be the recognition that all children develop differently, as individuals, at different speeds and in different ways. You also know, from your reading in this text, that there is a huge variety of factors that may impact upon that development. It can be seen, therefore, that whilst issues of safety, security and stability have a considerable impact upon childhood development, there are significant challenges for social work practice in identifying the impact and intervening to make a difference.

Daniel et al. (1999) suggest the following challenges:

- to identify whether what would have been a child's normal pattern of development has been interrupted or disrupted in some way;
- to establish whether the environment in which a child is living is likely to adversely affect their developmental path;
- to find ways to maximise the possibility of their attaining their developmental potential.

(1999, page 198)

You may have addressed some of these challenges in your 'good practice' points. Additionally, though, you may have been alerted, by the readings, to the importance of inter-professional and inter-agency practice when working with children. Hence, you may have included reference to information sharing, holistic assessment through integrated processes, such as the common assessment framework discussed earlier in the chapter and collective/collaborative practice. These notions of co-ordinated, integrated and comprehensive approaches to working with children are at the core of the contemporary national strategic direction for children's services. In the next activity, you are asked to explore the practical implications of this policy direction.

Finally, in your list of key 'good practice' points, you may also have included something about individual practitioner development, continued learning and reflective practice. These areas form the basis of this text and others in the series, as all aspects of professional social work practice should incorporate an awareness of self and personal professional development. There is further guidance about reflective practice in Chapter 7 of this book.

Practical implications and activities

Mills (2004, pages 53–4) concludes his research review by supporting key policy initiatives such as: *integration of education and children's social services; fostering a whole child approach in the education and children's services; information sharing across professional boundaries;* and *the importance of adequately resourcing inter-professional dialogue and training to support the above initiatives.*

Look at each of these four policy initiatives identified by Mills, and undertake some local research to find out exactly how these initiatives are being implemented in the locality in which you live. You may already work in a children's service and have ready access to some of this information. Otherwise, you could start by looking at the local authority's and the health authority's websites and exploring the range of links that they may provide. You could also contact your local authority directly and ask for copies of their local strategy documents in respect of services for children.

Chapter summary

This chapter and the following chapter together will assist you to develop your understanding about human life course development through childhood. Your studying through this chapter has been contextualised within the framework of current national policies, in particular the influential green paper *Every child matters* (DfES, 2003). In this chapter you will have worked through three main sections. The first set out to raise questions about how we understand the concept of childhood in our society. The latter two sections focused on two of the five key outcomes for children from the green paper (DfES, 2003), *be healthy* and *stay safe*. Within these sections extracts, analysis and reflective activities were provided to encourage you to think about how knowledge and understanding about childhood development interfaces with current thinking in respect of desired outcomes for children.

As described in the chapter introduction, this chapter should be read in conjunction with Chapter 3, which looks at the remaining three key outcomes: *enjoying and achieving; making a positive contribution;* and *achieving economic well-being.* Through these outcomes, Chapter 3 looks at cognitive and psychological development and also examines the impact of socio-economic issues on child development.

You will find that your learning from this chapter, along with the notes and responses you have made to the activities, will support your studies in the following chapters. Furthermore, it is recommended that you maintain a file of this work as evidence of your commitment to professional development and personal learning.

Annotated further reading and research

Arnold, C (1999) *Child development and learning 2–5 Years: Georgia's Story* London: Hodder & Stoughton. This book is written in easily readable story form, and tells the story of Georgia and her learning and development between the ages of two and five years of age. The author acknowledges that all children are unique, but this detailed case study of one child allows for comparison, analysis and debate about development through this stage of life. Throughout this book, Georgia's development, her behaviours and circumstances are explained through the use of a range of theoretical perspectives. The study utilised narrative approaches and observation in order to follow Georgia's story and through the book, readers get to know this real child, Georgia, and her family. The appendix at the end of the book, *Georgia's Gallery*, features a selection of photographs of Georgia with the people who were important to her during this phase of her life.

Abbott, L and Langston, A (eds) (2004) *Birth to three matters.* Buckingham: Open University Press.

Abbott and Langston provide a detailed exploration of the structure and framework of the *Birth to three matters* framework (DfES, 2002) which is discussed earlier in this chapter. Within their book, Abbott and Langston delve into national and international policy, case studies and contemporary research and thus underpin their very practical examples with a strong theoretical approach. If, after reading this chapter and the next, you are interested in looking further into early childhood development and related models of practice, you will find this text valuable.

Sure Start **www.surestart.gov.uk**. Sure Start is the government programme that aims to deliver a good start in life for every child. Sure Start integrates early education, childcare services, health, family support and community development. Their website provides an impressive range of links to other publications, research and other related websites.

Every child matters: Change for children **www.everychildmatters.gov.uk**. This website is a useful resource and starting point for information about a range of policy and strategy topics. It has four main sections that look at services and practice issues; strategy and governance, including different organisational structures; information for parents; and a link for children and young people with further links to other sites that provide help and advice for children.

IDeA Knowledge **www.idea-knowledge.gov.uk**. The IDeA Knowledge website provides examples of good practice from councils across England and Wales, and provides access to the IDeA's range of tools and services. The organisation supports work across the range of local authority services, and the site has an effective search facility. Thus, if you put the words *children* or *social work* into the search, it will locate a very useful list of research, good practice case-studies, policy and legislation to assist your studies.

3 Development in the middle years of childhood

ACHIEVING A SOCIAL WORK DEGREE

This chapter will begin to help you to meet the following National Occupational Standards:

Key Role 1: Prepare for, and work with, individuals, families, carers, groups and communities to assess their needs and circumstances.
- Assess needs and options to make a recommended course of action.

Key Role 2: Plan, carry out, review and evaluate social work practice, with individuals, families, carers, groups, communities and other professionals.
- Interact with individuals, families, carers, groups and communities to achieve change and development and to improve life opportunities.
- Work with groups to promote individual growth, development and independence.

Key Role 3: Support individuals to represent their needs, views and circumstances.
- Advocate with, and on behalf of, individuals, families, carers, groups and communities.

Key Role 6: Demonstrate professional competence in social work practice.
- Research, analyse, evaluate, and use current knowledge of best social work practice.

It will also introduce you to the following academic standards as set out in the social work subject benchmark statement:

3.1.1. Social work services and service users
- The social processes (associated with, for example, poverty, unemployment, poor health, disablement, lack of education and other sources of disadvantage) that lead to marginalisation, isolation and exclusion and their impact on the demand for social work services.
- The nature and validity of different definitions of, and explanations for, the characteristics and circumstances of service users and the services required by them.

3.1.2 The service delivery context
- The significance of legislative and legal frameworks and service delivery standards.

3.1.3 Values and ethics
- The moral concepts of rights, responsibility, freedom, authority and power inherent in the practice of social workers as moral and statutory agents.

3.1.4 Social work theory

- The relevance of psychological and physiological perspectives to understanding individual and social development and functioning.

- Research-based concepts and critical explanations from social work theory and other disciplines that contribute to the knowledge base of social work, including their distinctive epistemological status and application to practice.

- The relevance of sociological perspectives to understanding societal and structural influences on human behaviour at individual, group and community levels.

3.2.2 Problem solving skills
3.2.2.3. Analysis and synthesis
3.2.3. Communication skills

- Listen actively to others, engage appropriately with the life experiences of service users, understand accurately their viewpoint and overcome personal prejudices to respond appropriately to a range of complex personal and interpersonal situations.

3.2.4 Skills in working with others

- Involve users of social work services in ways that increase their resources, capacity and power to influence factors affecting their lives.

- Consult actively with others, including service users, who hold relevant information or expertise.

Introduction

In this chapter you will read about human development through the middle years of childhood from five years of age through to approximately 12 years of age. As stated previously, human development cannot be simplified or categorised into age-related segments. However, to facilitate clarity in this text, it has been necessary to divide childhood, using age, across Chapters 2 and 3. This chapter aims, therefore, to provide a continuation of your learning from the previous chapter, which focused on infants and young children from birth to five years to explore particular aspects of child development.

In accordance with the approach of this reflective reader, Chapters 2 and 3 aim to enable you to develop your knowledge of human development within the context of national policy and contemporary social work practice. This chapter and the preceding chapter have therefore been structured to take account of the five outcomes for children and young people taken from the green paper *Every child matters* (DfES, 2003) and the Children Act 2004. The Children Act 2004 provides the legal conduit for the green paper and the accompanying strategic development programme *Every child matters: Change for children* (DfES, 2004) (**www.everychildmatters.gov.uk**). Throughout this chapter you will be guided to read sections of the green paper and related policy documents in order to assist you to contextualise your learning. The outcomes framework published within *Every child matters: Change for children* (DfES, 2004) provides not only the five key outcomes, but also related aims for children. These are reproduced diagrammatically in Chapter 2. The final three outcomes provide the three sections of this chapter; *enjoying and achieving*; *making a positive contribution*; and *achieving economic well-being*.

In the first part of this chapter you will develop your knowledge of cognitive and psychological development in childhood. The middle section of the chapter then encourages you to reflect upon how children's views and experiences are heard, through the example of advocacy. The influence of increasing self-confidence and self-esteem on childhood development is relevant in this part of the chapter. The final section of the chapter offers a theoretical approach to aid the analysis of the effect of poverty and social deprivation on socioemotional development in childhood.

Throughout the chapter, reflective questions are presented to help you to:

- further your understanding of how individuals develop through learning and thinking in childhood;
- reflect on the significance of self-esteem and confidence, developed through meaningful participation and empowerment, on life course development;
- assess the potential impact of poverty and social deprivation on children's development.

One way in which you might study this chapter is to select sections which you feel are most relevant to your current learning needs, then read through the extract and analysis, undertake the activities in that section, take notes and record your reflections. However, you will develop a more holistic view of the developing child if you work through Chapter 2 and then this chapter in a methodical and structured way. It is not necessary or advisable to attempt to do this in one 'learning episode' or sitting, and therefore you might use the different sections of the chapter as natural break-off points during your learning. Whichever way you decide to structure your learning, it is suggested that you keep records which will provide an account of your progression for your own purposes, but will also serve as evidence of your commitment to continuing professional development. Further guidance and advice on different ways in which to record and share your learning are given in Chapter 7 of this book.

Cognitive development in the middle years of childhood

One of the strategic concerns of the *Every child matters* outcomes framework is that every child should *enjoy and achieve*. This objective focuses partly on learning and developing within school and partly on achieving personal and social development through, for example, the enjoyment of recreation. In order to improve educational outcomes and to work with children and young people towards personal, educational and social achievement, professionals need to understand how development of thinking, learning,

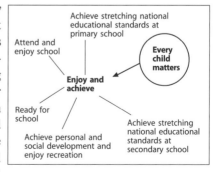

Figure 3.1

language and understanding in childhood are explained. The study of how people develop conceptual understanding, knowledge and use of language, the ability to problem-solve, reasoning, emotional stability, self-identity and moral understanding is known as *developmental psychology*. One particular area of developmental psychology is *cognitive developmental psychology* which focuses on the underlying processes and mechanisms that may determine how individuals process information and develop certain psychological behaviours, ways of thinking, learning and reasoning. Within the scope of this book, it is not possible to look at all the theories on cognitive development in childhood in detail. However, the extract provided offers an overview of the perspectives of three key theorists on the development of thinking and learning in childhood and also provides a brief comparative analysis of them.

The extract, studied together with the suggested pre-reading, the analysis and related activities, aims to stimulate your learning and reflection whilst also directing your further study. The reflective questions that you should refer to as you study this section are:

- how do different perspectives and theories explain cognitive development in middle childhood?
- how relevant and useful are these theories to contemporary society and social work practice?
- how does knowledge and understanding of cognitive development processes in middle childhood inform social work practice?

Preparatory reading

Before you read the extract, read:

- Department for Education and Skills (DfES) (2003) *Every child matters*, Cm 5860. London: Stationery Office. **www.dfes.gov.uk**. For this section it would be helpful if you could familiarise yourself again with Chapter 2 'Strong foundations', in particular pages 27–9.
- Crawford, K and Walker, J (2003) *Social work and human development*. Exeter: Learning Matters – pages 38–42 'The growing child – cognitive perspectives'.

Extract

Wood, D (1998) *How children think and learn*. 2nd edn. Oxford: Blackwell. pp37–9 'Piaget, Vygotsky and Bruner: a brief comparison and summary'.

Before moving on to the next chapter, I will summarize some of the main ideas we have just considered. Rather than simply repeat myself, I will try to re-examine these ideas whilst exploring a little more of the biography of the three main characters I have introduced.

I have outlined three main perspectives on the development of learning and thinking. These will be explored in more detail in the following pages. One view, which stems from Piaget's theory holds that all children pass through a series of stages before they construct the ability to perceive, reason and understand in mature, rational terms. In this view, teaching, whether through demonstration, explanation or asking questions, can only influence the course of intellectual development if the child is able to assimilate what is said and done. Assimilation, in turn, is constrained by the child's stage of development. This leads to a specific concept of learning 'readiness' and, as we shall see, holds out many implications for the design of curricula and the timing of formal instruction.

A second perspective, introduced by Vygotsky, shares some important areas of agreement with Piagetian theory, particularly an emphasis on *activity* as the basis for learning and for the development of thinking. However, it involves different assumptions about the relationship between talking and thinking. It entails a far greater emphasis on the role of communication, social interaction and instruction in determining the path of development. Vygotsky died in his late thirties in 1934. His death came after ten years of illness from tuberculosis. In that ten-year period, Vygotsky wrote about a hundred books and papers, many of which have only recently been published and translated into English. Many psychologists, including some of his own former students and colleagues, recognize that much of what he wrote was speculative and, in places, self-contradicting. Unlike Piaget, who worked on into his eighties and lived to see a dramatic expansion in the field of developmental psychology, Vygotsky did not have access to what has become a vast literature on child development. Consequently, whilst many of the ideas we will explore later in this book are consistent with his general position and were sometimes stimulated directly by it, we are left to guess at what Vygotsky himself might have had to say about them.

Bruner, influenced as I have already said by Vygotsky, was constructing the foundations of his theory of instruction in the 1960s when the assimilation of information theory into psychology was under way. Unlike both Vygotsky and Piaget, Bruner came to the study of child development after extensive research into adult thinking and problem-solving. Although sharing with Vygotsky a stress on the importance of culture and cultural history in the formation of mind, his background provided him with a more detailed sense of the *processes* involved in mature, socialized cognition. His theory, unlike either Piaget's or Vygotsky's, is grounded in the language of information theory. For instance, he entitled one of his early papers 'Going beyond the information given' (Bruner 1957). In this, he explored the nature of creative thinking and originality in terms of our ability not only to acquire information but also to 'go beyond' it by inventing codes and rules. Learning involves the search for pattern, regularity and predictability. Instruction serves to assist children in the formation and discovery of such patterns and rules. We return to a fuller discussion of these ideas in chapter 8.

Like Vygotsky, Bruner was convinced that social experience plays a major part in mental development, though his theory of the way in which social experience is involved in development differs from Vygotsky's account in a number of ways (not least by being informed by research findings that Vygotsky did not live to study). For example, throughout his writings on human development, Bruner laid considerable stress on the importance of acknowledging not only the role of culture and social interaction but also the influences of biology and evolution. He often drew parallels between the abilities of humans and other species when he theorized about the formation of mind: 'I take it as a working premise that growth cannot be understood without reference to human culture and primate evolution' (1968, p. 2). Vygotsky also acknowledged the importance of biological study in the creation of psychological theory. He distinguished between what he called the 'natural line' and the 'cultural line' in development. But he did not live to provide a synthesis of the two streams of growth. Indeed, unlike Bruner, he largely 'ignored' the natural, biological line in his desire to establish the importance of historical, social and cultural influences on human development (Wertsch, 1985, p. 8). You will find that discussions of the interplay between biology and social experience pervade this book. As we shall see, the last decade has seen a dramatic upsurge of interest in, and knowledge about, the innate capacities of the human infant and this has led to far more emphasis on the role of biological influences on human growth and development in recent theorizing about how children think and learn.

Looked at in one way, Bruner's theory stands between those of Paiget and Vygotsky. Like Piaget, Bruner emphasized the importance of biological and evolutionary constraints on human intelligence. At the same time, and more in sympathy with Vygotsky, he laid stress on the way in which culture forms and transforms the child's development, and he gave a more central role than Piaget did to social interaction, language and instruction in the formation of mind. Bruner employed the language of information processing in formulating his ideas and, in so doing, offered us an opportunity to integrate the findings from work on adult cognition with those arising from the study of children. All too often, cognitive psychologists who study adult intelligence ignore the process of development and education. They often leave one with the impression that mental activity springs, fully formed, out of developmental vacuum. Bruner, however, sought to ground his account of the 'processes of mind' in a theory of culture and growth, often drawing and building upon insights delivered by both Piaget and Vygotsky.

Piaget's theory, with its emphasis on the active, constructive nature of human development, is often referred to as a 'constructivist' approach. Whilst Bruner also accepted the image of children as active architects of their own understanding he, in company with Vygotsky, stressed the role of social interaction and cultural practices in shaping the course of human development. Their approach is often referred to as 'social constructivism'. As we shall see in the next chapter, both of these theoretical perspectives have been extended and modified over the past decade. They have also come under critical scrutiny from those who hold that nature and biology play a far more crucial role in shaping human destiny than either of these approaches allow.

Analysis

In the middle years of childhood, some of the most significant areas of growth and change are seen in psychosocial, cognitive, emotional and moral development (Schofield, 2006). The extract from Wood (1998) offers only a very brief comparison and summary of Lev Vygotsky's (1896–1934), Jean Piaget's (1896–1980) and Jerome Bruner's (1915–the present) perspectives on how children learn and develop their thinking. However, despite only being a short extract, it should provide a useful starting point, or revision point, for additional reading, exploration and examination of how children's cognitive development is understood. Further into his book, Wood (1998) explores how these perspectives have developed in more recent times and considers the ways in which these theories have influenced approaches to education and working with children. For example, Karmiloff-Smith (cited in Wood, 1998, page 43) offers an approach which was originally developed from the work of Piaget, but has moved away from the notion of staged-development to one of a 'modular' mind. This way of understanding cognitive development in childhood suggests that learning and growth is almost segmented into distinct domains. In this way Karmiloff-Smith's explanation can account for children who perhaps appear very developed and advanced in one area, for example language acquisition, but are less developed in another area, for example problem solving.

It is recommended that you explore these theories further to increase your knowledge of the theories that underpin professional practice with children. It is important, though, that as you study any theory, you are mindful that theories are always open to interpretation. For example, Wood's comparison and further analysis in his book is just one way, or a part of one way, of understanding the perspectives of these theorists, and there are, in fact, many different interpretations of these theories. Having read the extract, you may find it helpful to your learning to attempt to summarise Wood's interpretation of each approach. One way of doing this would be to complete a table with headings that you could then try to fill in. So, for example, you can extract that Piaget's approach is known as *constructivist*, whilst Bruner and Vygotsky are labelled as *social constructivists*. (Constructivist theories of learning are based on the premise that individuals are active participants in *constructing* their learning through experiences, reflection and meaning while social constructivists add the significance of culture, society and social interaction in influencing learning.) You could then add some of the similarities and differences that the author highlights, such as how each theorist interprets the importance of activity. An example of similarity between the approaches is where Wood notes that all three theorists, Vygotsky, Piaget and Bruner, acknowledge, to some degree, the potential influence of biological and/or evolutionary factors on cognitive development. This links to the 'nature–nurture' debate, which you read about in the first section of Chapter 2 of this text.

As you work through these theories, consider whether you feel that they do offer a relevant and helpful explanation of how children develop their thinking, learning and reasoning in today's society. Are there, from your perspective, issues that they do not cover, or that are not adequately addressed? For example, using the pre-reading materials for this section, you will see that the green paper *Every child matters* explicitly outlines the importance of raising the attainment of minority ethnic pupils as *there is evidence to show that the performance of pupils from certain minority ethnic backgrounds lags considerably behind that of their peers* (DfES, 2003, page 28). Do these theories help us to understand why this might be so and what we might do about it? Paludi (2002, page 98) explains how the learning culture and environment may impact adversely upon children from some cultures. She gives the example of how children from some cultures, for example Native American, Southeast Asian and Mexican American backgrounds, are used to working co-operatively within an ethos of community learning. Yet in a traditionally western learning environment, where competition, individual learning, achievement and performance may be valued, these children could be disadvantaged, considered to be cheating, or feel confused by what is expected of them.

Another significant aspect of childhood in our society, that is not overtly or specifically considered in this extract, is *play*. The summary by Wood does underline the importance of social activity, experience and interaction in influencing cognitive development and play is, of course, all of those things. Play has been recognised as highly important by a range of professionals and academic researchers (Bodrova and Leong, 2003). Daniel et al. (1999) state that watching the way in which a child plays can help to inform us about their developmental progress.

> The young child who is allowed to explore their senses of hearing, touch, sight and smell is more securely based in the world and this is a sound building block for later healthy development.

and

> In play children can explore their own potential, their skills and limitations and, with support, can gain enjoyment in extending themselves. (Daniel et al., 1999, page 179)

Bodrova and Leong (2003, page 50) also consider that play facilitates development stating that *with the right approach, a plain white hat and a plate full of yarn spaghetti can contribute to a young child's cognitive development.* In respect of professional practice, Daniel et al. (1999, page 179) argue that play not only helps us to understand and progress a child's development, but is also a *powerful therapeutic tool.* Whilst recognising the significance of play, it is also vital that you are aware that play is culturally specific. For example, research undertaken by Currer (1991), herself a social worker, into Central Asian family life found different values and concepts in relation to play, beliefs and children's activities. Currer's research and findings will provide interesting and thought-provoking reading if you are working, or considering work, with young children, particularly in respect of assumptions, pre-judgements and discriminatory practice.

Personal reflections

Reflect on your own learning during childhood and your middle school years. Alternatively, if you are a parent or carer of children in this age group, think about how they are learning, progressing, achieving and developing. Then look back at the ways in which Piaget, Vygotsky and Bruner explain cognitive development in childhood. Do you feel that any one of these theories provides a more comprehensive, relevant and appropriate way of understanding how children develop their learning and thinking? If so, write down why you think so, and how their approach helps to explain the example you have in mind. If you find it more difficult to agree with one particular perspective, also record why this might be so. You could extend your reflections further, by considering whether the theories are also comprehensive enough to explain how children from differing cultures and backgrounds learn and develop.

Comment

Your personal reflections on the above activity will be just that, 'personal'. What you have been doing within this activity, and also as you read the analysis on the extract, is applying theory and critiquing it. Analysing theory, deconstructing and critiquing it are all ways in which we start to consider the application of and integration of theory into our practice. The Department for Education and Skills (DfES, 2005a, page 12) highlights the importance of *knowing how to use theory and experience to reflect upon, think about and improve your practice* within the *Common core of skills and knowledge* required for everyone working with children, young people, their families and carers.

Practical implications and activities

The government guidance for the *Common Assessment Framework (CAF) for children and young people: Practitioners' guide* (DfES, 2006) states that the *CAF is aimed at children who need additional support to enable them to progress* satisfactorily to the five outcomes. The outcome *'enjoy and achieve'* is relevant to cognitive development and relates to school achievement and enjoying recreational activities, alongside working with parents and carers to enable them to support learning. As a social work practitioner you may be called upon to work with a range of other professionals to undertake this form of integrated assessment with a child and its carers. In what ways do you feel that your knowledge of cognitive development theories and the significance of social interaction and play, can inform your assessment practice? You might consider the role that professionals from other disciplines might have in the assessment process and how your specialist knowledge and skills can complement and add to the holistic understanding of a child's circumstances.

Psychological development in childhood

Following on from your reading on cognitive development in the middle years of childhood, in this section of the chapter, you will now extend that learning to consider how children develop self-confidence and self-esteem through participation and involvement. The *Every child matters* (DfES, 2003) stated outcome *make a positive contribution* covers a range of aims which broadly set out aspirations for children's and young people's behaviour and involvement in their

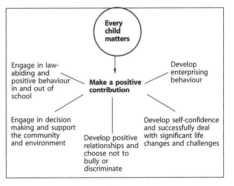

Figure 3.2

communities. However, in the green paper, the DfES (2003, page 78) specifically highlights the significance of involving children in *the planning, delivery and evaluation of policies* related to the health, education and social care services provided by a range of agencies. This is further reinforced in the *Every child matters: Change for children* (DfES, 2004, page 9) strategy document, where the specific aims within the outcomes framework state that, through making a positive contribution, young people will *develop self-confidence and successfully deal with significant life changes and challenges.*

Through your reading, reflection and analysis on the extract provided in this section, consider how, in professional practice, the positive contribution and participation of children and young people might be genuinely and meaningfully enabled. Then consider how such participation might contribute to their life course, and, specifically, psychological development. The suggested questions to think about and reflect upon as you study this section are:

- what are the underlying values, principles and beliefs that will enable an effective and genuine participative approach?
- what are the practical challenges to enabling meaningful participation of children and young people in areas that impact upon their lives?
- how do we know that we are effectively enabling meaningful participation of children and young people in areas that impact upon their lives?
- in what ways does participation enable psychological development in childhood?

Preparatory reading

Before you read the extract, read:

- Department of Health (DoH) (2004) *National Service Framework for children, young people and maternity services.* London: Stationery Office. **www.doh.gov.uk**
  It is suggested that you familiarise yourself with Standard 3 (page 15) which focuses on taking account of the views of children, young people and their families. This is also another opportunity for you to increase your awareness of the range of cross-governmental guidance throughout which the theme of enabling participation can be identified.

- DfES (2001) *Learning to listen: core principles for the involvement of children and young people.* Nottingham: DfES Publications Centre.
  This guidance was developed to provide authorities and professionals working with children and young people with guidance, through a framework of core principles, on how to plan the effective participation of children and young people in policy and service delivery. The principles are developed from Article 12 of the United Nations Convention on the Rights of the Child (to which the UK is a signatory). (DfES, 2001, page 3). This document is available to order in hard copy, or download from the Internet at **www.everychildmatters.gov.uk/participation.**

- Department of Health (DoH) (2002) *Listening, hearing and responding.* London: Stationery Office. **www.doh.gov.uk**
  This government document builds upon the *Learning to listen* document above and is labelled as an *action plan* showing how the government intend to increase communication and involvement of children and young people. It raises the important issue of confidentiality and consent within consultation (page 21) and provides a range of examples of work and structures already in place that are seen as enabling mechanisms.

Selected extracts from

Dalrymple, J (2005) Constructions of child and youth advocacy: Emerging issues in advocacy practice. *Children and society*, 19, pp3–5, 15.

The development of child and youth advocacy has been informed by varying theoretical perspectives and in the last decade has been increasingly incorporated into policy and legislation for young people in receipt of welfare services. Through examining the varying perspectives of young people, advocates and commissioners of advocacy services it can be seen that although there is some consensus about how advocacy should be provided, the construction of advocacy by adults may have a significant impact on how it is experienced by young people. This paper draws on material from five advocacy projects to examine how advocacy is constructed by those involved in the provision and receipt of services. It argues that there is a danger that the construction of advocacy in an adult proceduralised way is likely to compromise its potential to challenge the structures that deny young people opportunities to participate in decision making about their lives.

Recognition of the need for vulnerable young people to have access to independent advocacy when they feel that they are not being listened to or heard has led to a proliferation of advocacy services in England and Wales in the last decade. Advocacy has primarily developed for young people in receipt of welfare services with the acknowledgement that adult systems set up to make decisions about their lives have, in the past, failed to provide opportunities for their participation (Department of Health, 2000; Utting, 1997; Waterhouse, 2000). Organisations have developed both locally and nationally and the pioneering works of many have served to develop knowledge about child and youth advocacy practice (see for example Preston, 1995; Noon, 2000; Scutt, 1995; Templeton and Kemmis, 1998; Wyllie, 1999; Boylan and Boylan, 1998; Dalrymple and Hough, 1995). However, although young people in all local authorities have access to some form of advocacy support, knowledge about them is limited (Children's Rights Officers and Advocates (CROA), 1998) and only more recently has there been any systematic inquiry into the provision of advocacy (Clarke, 2003; Kelly, 2002).

In this paper I aim to contribute to a contemporary understanding of the nature of child and youth advocacy through analysis of data obtained from five studies. The paper begins with a brief overview of the issues surrounding children's status and a summary of advocacy provision within child welfare services. It will then draw on material from the studies to illustrate how advocacy is constructed by young people, advocates and commissioners of advocacy services. The studies represent a very small proportion of young people receiving welfare services. Furthermore on the whole they only represent articulate young people or those with articulate carers. However they still raise a number of issues about the nature of advocacy and in presenting the material I have addressed two broad questions.

- What do the studies tell us about advocacy – that is how is advocacy constructed and given meaning by the actors (young people and advocates) through the process?
- How does that knowledge contribute to developing a discourse about child and youth advocacy – that is what are the meanings and interpretations of practice held by those involved in it?

For simplicity of presentation in the paper the term 'young people' will be used to refer to children and young people.

The need for advocacy

The powerless position of children as an identifiable group (Mayall, 2002), and the disadvantages faced by young people who are denied fundamental rights because of poverty, ethnicity, disability, sexuality, immigration status or geography (Children's Rights Development Unit, 1994), and other social differences such as religion, mental health, gender or care status, means that they may struggle to find opportunities to develop competence and confidence (Hart, 1992). An ideal community will nurture families and children and often the advocacy of parents or other natural advocates will resolve problems and difficulties that arise in their lives. But there are many situations 'where young people and their natural advocates will require assistance from more formal advocacy services' (Office of the Ombudsman of British Colombia, 1993, p. 14).

Research and inquiries indicate that despite legislative requirements to involve young people in decisions about their lives many do not feel that they have a voice in processes such as reviews (Boylan, 1996), or case conferences (Farnfield, 1997) and find complaints procedures difficult to access and intimidating to use (Aiers and Kettle, 1998; Wallis and Frost, 1998; Waterhouse, 2000). They have little confidence in child protection procedures, preferring to use confidential helplines than approach statutory agencies (McLeod, 1999). They often do not feel that they have been listened to, taken seriously or respected (Boylan and Boylan, 1998; Butler and Williamson, 199; Wattam and Woodward, 1996). Furthermore, Wattam and Parton suggest, professional responses in the UK are predicated on a particular view of childhood 'which is brought to the attention of the state when it is obviously contravened' (1999, p. 3). For example, rather than interrogate the causes of sexual violence to children or young people, constraints in the name of protection are imposed, with the victim and the family coming under scrutiny. This desire for the 'preservation' of childhood may be engendered by moral panics that accompany the actions of young people such as Robert Thompson and John Venables when they killed James Bulger, provoking responses that demonised them (Goldson, 2001).

In the last decade a 'new' sociology of childhood has emerged (James and Prout, 1997) which has helped raise the status of childhood (Mayall, 2002, p. 178). Articulating the position of children as 'social actors' such theorists are developing a sociological perspective that has been described as a theory of advocacy because it is committed to the purposes and interests of children: a theory for rather than of children. While these theories are not without their critics (Lavalette and Cunningham, 2002) they have stimulated debate concerning the status of young people in an adult world, highlighting ambivalent attitudes to them either as 'victims' to be protected or 'villains' needing control (Goldson, 2002) and increasing opportunities for their participation (Willow, 2002; Thomas, 2000). However this does not necessarily mean that approaches to policy and practice are more child centred and in some respects, especially for certain social groups, their position has become more marginal (Wattam and Parton, 1999).

The role of the advocate within such discourses is equally complex. Definitions of advocacy rely on concepts of childhood and on vulnerability. Both the status and the circumstances of childhood are relevant here – young people can be vulnerable but become vulnerable because of the social mechanisms which impinge on their lives. In the provision of services 'expert' knowledge in relation to vulnerable young people is used to control and act on them as targets of intervention (Sohng, 1998). By standing alongside them advocates are challenging dominant discourses about the nature of childhood and thus are confronting the monopoly of knowledge by 'experts' about the capacity of young people to speak for themselves. Advocacy services could therefore be described as empowerment projects (Parsons, 1998), or as tools for critical practitioners to confront the oppression of young people by adults, adult professionals and institutions. This is not to deny that young people have the capacity for individual or collective resistance but to acknowledge that, in certain situations, they need support to enable them to come to voice.

Final thoughts

The National Standards for Advocacy (Department of Health, 2002; Welsh Assembly Government, 2003) clearly state that it should be led by young people. However advocacy is constructed by many stakeholders. While young people can clearly identify how advocacy can enable them to gain control in decision making processes affecting their personal lives, they are less able to influence the systems. The danger for the development of advocacy is that by standing alongside young people advocates can also become controlled by commissioners, who subscribe to protectionist discourses. As knowledge about how systems oppress young people is made public, health and social care practitioners may feel threatened, not just by reports or inquiries, but by the daily experiences of advocates with young people. Advocacy, informed by a rights discourse, can enable young people to influence planning processes and develop skills and confidence in the process. However, if the development of advocacy services are to radically change policy and practice and challenge discourses which maintain the status of young people as a minority group, they need to be constructed from the perspective of young people and resist construction by commissioners of services in an adult proceduralised way.

Analysis

This extract is made up of selected sections from a journal article that, following analysis of research data, considers the importance, not only of listening to children and enabling their participation, but also of understanding how children and young people construct key concepts, such as advocacy. In the article, through her discussion of perspectives on advocacy, Dalrymple (2005) leads the reader to reflect upon the importance of understanding children's perspectives on the different influences on their lives, before considering how their participation might be genuine and effective. In this way, as professionals, we need to ask ourselves what notions, such as advocacy, actually mean to children and young people. Additionally, Dalrymple (2005, page 5) argues that our approach to working with children, for example in respect of the role of the advocate, depends upon our adult perception and construction of childhood. The social construction and meanings attached to childhood are discussed in the first section of Chapter 2; you may find it useful to look back at that section.

You should also note that Dalrymple's argument is underpinned by a *rights discourse*. This means that children's rights as citizens are acknowledged and that there is a commitment to seeing and respecting children and young people as individuals who have valid views and opinions and are able to make informed judgements. To develop your understanding of a rights discourse in respect of children and young people, you could visit the website of the Children's Rights Alliance for England **www.crae.org.uk**.

You should also ensure that you are aware of, and have read, the UN Convention on the Rights of the Child, which is the first legally binding international policy to incorporate the full range of human rights – civil, cultural, economic, political and social. The full text of the convention is most easily accessed from UNICEF via their website **www. unicef.org**.

Additionally, research and literature inform us that children's psychological development, particularly the development of confidence, self-esteem, self-image, identity development and self-awareness is influenced by their interactions with others in the world around them (Berryman et al., 2002; Quinton, 2006). Furthermore, the opportunities to develop in this way will be reduced where such interactions are not effective, for example where children are powerless, disadvantaged or oppressed (Hart, cited in Dalrymple, 2005, page 4). The significance of social interaction in developing an understanding of 'self' is also considered by Berryman et al. (2002).

> It is impossible to be aware of ourselves, and to have a self-image, without being aware of others. How we see ourselves is affected by how others see us and also by how we think others see us. These ideas (of who or what we are) are socially defined, so self-awareness is a social concept.
>
> (Berryman et al., 2002, page 51)

You have seen in the pre-reading and earlier discussion, how national policy guidance also supports the view that participation and meaningful interaction are ways in which professionals can enable the development of psychological and emotional well-being in children and young people. The document that you have been directed to as pre-reading for this section states that *there is already a lot of evidence . . . that involving children and young people in the planning, delivery and evaluation of government services brings benefits* and that *Good participation opportunities produce more confident and resilient young people* (DfES, 2001: 6).

There is, therefore, consensus that the genuine participation of children and young people in all areas of society that affect their lives and life courses is their right and is a good thing, not only for the children's own psychological well-being and development, but also for the development of services and society. However, Dalrymple, in the extract and, more extensively, in the full article, provides us with much 'food for thought' and reflective material about how we, as adults and individuals working with children, might make this real and effective. For example, if we begin to try to understand the differing perspectives of children and adults on a range of concepts that impact upon our practice, we also need to understand the impact of culture, cognitive and psychological development on those perceptions and understandings. O'Hagan (1999) draws attention to the centrality of language and understanding and how issues of communication can result in discriminatory power imbalance. This is not dissimilar to the issues of power imbalance that Dalrymple raises, but clearly where there are cultural and/or language differences between worker and the child or their carers, this will compound the complexities of vulnerability and differing constructions that are described by Dalrymple.

Personal reflections

Dalrymple (2005, page 4) cites the work of a range of authors to evidence that *despite legislative requirements to involve young people in decisions about their lives many do not feel that they have a voice in processes* that are likely to direct affect them. However, you have seen from the discussion above and your reading that it is not always straightforward to enable the meaningful participation of young people, either at the level of working with the individual, or at a service level. As you reflect upon the concept of participation and its influence in the psychological development of children and young people, complete the following task. If you are a practitioner, make a list of the different practical methods, either from your own practice, or from service or team procedures, that are in place to enable children and young people to be listened to, heard and responded to. In other words, in what ways are children empowered to influence services? Also, as you make this list, in the light of your reading of the analysis above, attempt to critique those methods. How genuinely effective are they? Then look back on your list and consider, in an ideal world, what additional, innovative means you could incorporate. If you do not have direct practice experience, start your list by thinking of practical ways in which you might work to enable the meaningful participation of young people.

Comment

Effective communication and engagement with children, young people, their families and carers is one of the fundamental areas of the *Common core of skills and knowledge* (DfES, 2005a. page 6) that all people working with children, young people and their families, should develop. Perhaps, the starting point, particularly for the second part of this activity might seem quite obvious. Asking young people directly the ways in which they would feel most comfortable and confident would be one way to begin to engage with their perspectives and views. However, even within this method, the issues of language, culture and differing constructions must be considered if you are to reduce power imbalances and ensure anti-oppressive practice. You must be aware too that each individual has different needs and preferences in relation to communication, so a range of different methods is needed. The DfES also detail a range of skills that you will need in order to ensure effective communication, such as the ability to listen, demonstrate empathy and develop relationships, using non-verbal communication and building trust and mutual respect (DfES, 2005a). You may have thought of many innovative strategies, including some of the following: use of websites; chat rooms; advisory groups; text messaging; and advocacy. Essentially though, whatever methods you select, in consultation with children themselves, you need to ensure that they reflect the developmental stage of the child, their understanding, culture, language, self-esteem and confidence. Above all, to be mutually beneficial, participation should be enjoyable and rewarding.

Practical implications and activities

Throughout chapters 2 and 3 you have been guided to national strategy, legislation and policy documents that incorporate, in different ways, the desired outcome of increased involvement and participation of children and young people at all levels of health and social care services. For this activity, you are asked to investigate how these national objectives are being implemented in your local area. You could use the Internet (all local authorities, trusts and health agencies have websites), your local library or local service access points to try and ascertain what is being done locally to ensure that services are *listening, hearing and responding* to the views and needs of children and young people.

Given your reading of the extract above, the good practice examples that are cited in the pre-reading suggestions for this section and your developing understanding of psychological development in childhood, critique the examples that you find in your locality. How far, for example, do they enable and empower all children to have their voices heard? Or do they, as Dalrymple (2005, page 4) states, *only represent articulate young people or those with articulate carers*? Furthermore, in the extract Dalrymple (2005) raises the notion of *a culture of advocacy*. In your investigation of local mechanisms to enable children's participation, how far do you sense a *culture of meaningful participation* being developed? How do you judge and measure the success and effectiveness of this?

The impact of poverty and deprivation on childhood development

The first chapter of *Every child matters* (DfES, 2003), 'The challenge', sets out the policy challenges and goals for children and young people. Within the chapter, there is acknowledgement that *there is a big gap between the development of children from different socio-economic groups* (ibid, page 18) and that *when children enter primary school, children from poorer backgrounds start to fall behind children from higher income families* (ibid, page 19).

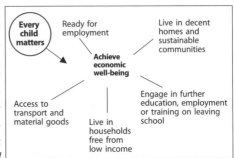

Figure 3.3

This final section of Chapter 3, considers the *Every child matters* (DfES, 2003) strategic outcome, *achieve economic wellbeing*. In particular, you will be encouraged to reflect upon the possible impact of poverty and deprivation on children's development. Within this, the extract and analysis offer you the opportunity to consider how, in social work practice, you might develop an understanding of the experience of children from different socio-economic backgrounds and how their environment might influence their life course development. Whilst this chapter has focused on the middle years of childhood, the discussion and issues raised in this section can be related to developmental issues across the whole of childhood. As you study this section, you will also see how the issues of poverty and deprivation provide a useful concluding section to chapters 2 and 3, in that environmental and economic factors potentially pervade all the aspects of childhood development that have been considered throughout the chapters. Thus, the reflective prompts suggested earlier in Chapters 2 and in this chapter are also relevant as you read the preparatory material, extract and analysis which follows. Additionally, the questions that you should think about as you read through this section of the chapter are:

- in what ways might poverty and social deprivation impact upon child development?
- how can I ensure that I understand the experience of children in different situations in society?
- what does this tell me about my social work practice?

Before you start reading through this section of this chapter, consider the following statistics which have been selected from the many facts and figures available about children and their families in our society. Reflect on what these figures might tell us about the lives and experiences of children in England and the significance of the professional support and care that they receive. The statistics have been taken from the New Policy Institute's Monitoring Poverty and Social Exclusion website, which is supported by the Joseph Rowntree Foundation.

- The number of children living in low income households was 3½ million in 2003/04. This represents a drop of ¾ million since 1996/97.
- Children are one-and-a-half times more likely to live in a low income household as adults.
- A half of all lone parents are in low income households, two-and-a-half times the rate for couples with children.
- Almost 2 million children live in workless households.
- The Government's short term target for child poverty is to reduce the numbers by a quarter in the period 1998/99 to 2004. Achieving this will require a fall of 400,000 in the year 2004/05.

www.poverty.org.uk

Statistical information of this type should always be further interrogated and analysed as it only provides a 'snapshot' of information. Information of this type is also always being updated and re-interpreted. Another web-based resource that provides a range of statistical data and related information is the Child Poverty Action Group site at **www.cpag.org.uk**.

Preparatory reading

Before you read this extract, read:

- Seden, J (2006) Frameworks and theories in Aldgate, J, Jones, D, Rose, W and Jeffery, C (eds) *The developing world of the child*. London: Jessica Kingsley, pages 35–54.
  In this chapter, Seden outlines a range of theoretical frameworks that are used to explain children's life course development. Pages 38–9 are of particular relevance to the extract and the subsequent analysis, as Seden examines *ecological thinking, theories and frameworks.*

- Crawford, K and Walker, J (2003) *Social work and human development*. Exeter: Learning Matters. Chapter 2, pages 19–20.
  If you feel unfamiliar with Bronfenbrenner's theory of ecological development, you

will find a straightforward explanation within Chapter 2 of this text. There is also a diagram which may help you to conceptualise the framework envisaged by Bronfenbrenner.

- HM Treasury (2004) *Child poverty review.* London: The Stationery Office. **www-hm-treasury.gov.uk**
  This government publication examines welfare reform and public services in the light of the government's long-term goal of halving child poverty by 2010 and eradicating it by 2020. Chapter 5 is particularly relevant to the discussion here as it considers how public services contribute to tackling child poverty and improving life chances for poor children.

Selected extracts

Eamon, M K (2001) The effects of poverty on children's socioemotional development: An ecological systems analysis. *Social work*, 46(3), pp256–66.

Bronfenbrenner's process-person-context-time model is used to examine theories that explain the adverse effects of economic deprivation on children's socio-emotional development. In his model, each of five structures of the ecological environment – microsystems, mesosystems, exosystems, macrosystems, and chronosystems – is subsumed within the next higher level. Theories of the effects of poverty on proximal processes in the microsystem of the family have the most research support, but processes in other microsystems such as the peer group and school and in other levels of the ecological environment may also explain the relation between economic deprivation and children's socioemotional functioning. Social work practice and policy implications are drawn from the analysis.

Summary
The nested structures of the ecological environment proposed by Bronfenbrenner's process-person-context-time model provide a useful framework for examining theories of the effects of economic deprivation on children's socioemotional development. Within the microsystem of the home, stress-coping theory and family process models frequently are used to explain the socioemotional developmental effects of poverty. The stressful life events or chronic strains caused by economic deprivation appear to affect children's socioemotional functioning by eroding parental coping behaviors, creating psychological distress and marital discord, and resulting in parenting practices that are uninvolved, inconsistent, emotionally unresponsive, and harsh. This review suggests that practitioners who work with low-income families and children with socioemotional problems should assess parental psychological distress, coping behaviors, the quality of the marital or partner relationship, and parenting practices to assist in selecting appropriate interventions.

Parent–child interactions do not always account for the relation between poverty and children's socioemotional functioning. Poverty may result in children's socioemotional problems by impeding or influencing peer relations, attending low-quality schools, or being exposed to unsupportive school environments. Assessing interactions within the peer group and school also may provide valuable assessment information. Child characteristics such as a difficult temperament, gender, and health problems (chronic health conditions, undernutrition, and elevated lead levels) may have independent effects on socioemotional functioning or may intensify the influence of poverty. Assessing and providing appropriate interventions for these problems may improve children's socioemotional functioning.

Poverty may affect children's socioemotional development in mesosystems (such as linkages between home and school) and in exosystems (the parents' social support group and community). Increasing support in parents' social support networks and communities may decrease parental psychological distress and improve parenting practices. Assessing the child's exposure to violence and associations with deviant peers may also provide information for intervening at the individual, family, or community level.

Consistent with Bronfenbrenner's conceptualization of macrosystems, researchers and social workers frequently recognize that developmental processes may be contingent on particular culture or subculture, including shared beliefs and knowledge, and no available economic resources and opportunities. Although whether the processes by which poverty affects the socioemotional development of children vary by race or ethnicity or culture is yet to be determined, social policies that increase access to economic resources and quality housing, neighborhoods, schools, nutrition, and health care are likely to enhance proximal processes in the more immediate system levels and result in better developmental outcomes.

Chronosystems, historical and life events, and individual change across the life span, also have important influences on child development. Although chronic poverty has detrimental effects on children's socioemotional development, income loss appears to be particularly disruptive to parent–child interactions. Social policies that educate families concerning these risks and ensure families access to mental health services and economic resources may help to stabilize the parent–child interactions that appear to have detrimental effects on the socioemotional functioning of both younger and older children.

As Bronfenbrenner observed, the processes by which economic deprivation affects children's socioemotional development are multiple and complex. Given the complexities and multiple paths by which poverty can affect the socioemotional development of children, an ecological systems model provides an appropriate framework to guide research, assessment procedures, and selection of appropriate interventions for poor families and children experiencing socioemotional problems.

Analysis

This extract consists of the initial abstract, or brief summary, and the final concluding summary of the journal article. You will find that you need to have an understanding of Bronfenbrenner's ecological systems model in order to fully comprehend the approach and theoretical basis that Eamon uses for her evaluation of the impact of poverty on children's development. You should note too, that Eamon focuses particularly on children's socioemotional development. However through your pre-reading and any further study in this area, you will become aware that there is extensive research that demonstrates that children who grow up in deprivation are at increased risk of a range of other developmental disadvantages, for example in their health, educational and language attainment (**www.nspcc.org.uk**) See also Department of Health (2001a). Dowling et al. (2006) suggest that poverty may affect child development in two ways: firstly its impact on parenting capacity (this is also referred to by Eamon in the extract); and secondly, it may lead to discrimination, stigmatisation and social exclusion.

In order to explore these concepts, Eamon takes the reader through the different levels of analysis and considers the models, frameworks and theoretical approaches that are used to explain the effects of environmental factors at that level. You may need to extend your studies by reading about some of the particular models that Eamon refers to, such as *family process models*. Eamon also makes connections to social work practice by suggesting the implications of the theoretical analysis for the actions of practitioners. Seden (2006, page 35) in the text suggested for pre-reading, argues that *frameworks and theories of practice are not separate from the tasks of practice*. If you go back through the extract you will see a number of references to direct social work practice tasks, for example assessment, community and network support, which enable parenting skills and risk assessment – you may have found others.

A systems perspective, as taken by Eamon to structure the analysis in her article, starts from a social focus, exploring people's social situations, rather than starting from a focus on the individual (Payne, 2005, page 142). In Chapter 6 of this book, the potential debate concerning social work focusing on social issues, as opposed to starting with the individual, is discussed further. Eamon's ecological approach is also adopted by Dowling et al. (2006, page 141) who argue that it enables *understanding of the mutual influence between children's development, the circumstances of their family, and the environment and neighbourhood in which the families live out their daily lives.* Additionally, you might consider whether Eamon is taking a developmental or an ecological perspective. The developmental perspective refers to an approach which views a sense of progression and increasing complexity (Aldgate, 2006, page 20) for each individual child as they grow up. *It is increasingly recognised that alongside a developmental perspective, there is an ecological perspective of children's development* (Aldgate, 2006, page 23), so it could be argued that Eamon has integrated both of these approaches to assist our understanding of the impact of poverty on Children's socioemotional development.

In the extract Eamon also underlines the complexity of attempting to understand and explain how economic deprivation affects the children's development. In particular she raises the potential effects of a range of other variables, such as health, ethnicity and culture. Potentially there is also another factor which contributes to and perhaps underpins, or is the starting point, for all of this complexity. Payne (2005, page 22) discusses the *social construction of social work* and the *social construction of social work theory*. He suggests that:

> Theory for practice will inevitably respond to current social realities, so that present interests and concerns colour it. Yet is also reflects the histories of theoretical, occupational and service context. (ibid)

As you reflect on what Payne's statements mean, in relation to the theories and resultant practice outlined by Eamon in the extract, you should attempt to think through what might have 'coloured' or influenced Eamon's work. So, for example, how far have social work professional values and ethics informed these ideas? Or, how far have political or ideological stances influenced the theories chosen and the practices described? Furthermore, given the focus of this reflective reader, how far do these social constructions influence our understanding and the meanings we attach to the experience and developmental needs of children in our society?

Personal reflections

Seden (2006, page 36) states that *professionals need to be able to reflect consciously how their internalised values and theories are influencing their practice. This includes judging what theoretical knowledge is relevant.* In the analysis I have also suggested that it is important to consider the underlying influences on theory and related practice. This is, therefore, an opportunity for you to reflect upon your personal and professional values and the potential wider influences on theory and practice with regard to how you develop your understanding of the impact of poverty and deprivation on life course development in childhood. You could start from analysing whether you feel the theoretical approach in the reading materials is relevant and applicable, then consider whether it informs your practice and if so, how.

Comment

It is likely that as you read through the extract and the analysis, you will have been, possibly without realising it, actually working through this reflective activity. However, in undertaking the activity now, it is intended that you make explicit your personal underlying values, assumptions and the social work professional values and ethics that impact upon your practice. Additionally, as you integrate theory, alongside the policy drivers and practice tasks and models, you should be able to critique some of the wider political, social, cultural and ideological influences on social work practice and our understanding of children in our society. With that developing critical, analytical understanding, reflect back on the questions at the beginning of this section and consider your responses to them now.

Practical implications and activities

In the previous chapter you studied the Common Assessment Framework (CAF) (DfES, 2006), and its elements and domains, which provide a mechanism for drawing together a range of information about a child's development, their carers and the support available to them. You may find it helpful to refer back to Chapter 2 before working on this activity. One of the domains of the Common Assessment Framework, which is an integral element of the strategic direction outlined in *Every child matters*, is *the impact of wider family and environmental elements on the child's development and on the capacity of their parents* (DfES, 2006, page 17). For this activity, reflect upon the extract by Eamon, your pre-reading and the analysis in this section of the chapter, then consider how you, as a social work practitioner, in very practical terms, can ensure that your assessment of this aspect of a child and their carers' lives is enabling and comprehensive. What are the questions and explorations that you would want to make? How would you listen to and involve the child and their family or carers? Who else would you involve and how? Within this domain, the CAF guidance (DfES, 2006, page 31/32) suggests the following elements are considered: family history; functioning; well-being; wider family; housing; employment; financial considerations; social and community elements; resources and education. You may find that these elements provide a useful structure to your thinking.

Chapter summary

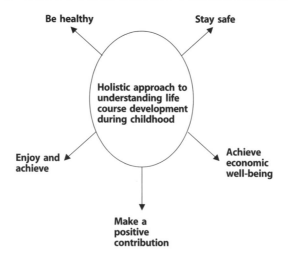

Adapted from *Every child matters: Change for children* (DfES, 2004)

Figure 3.4 Taking an holistic approach

Chapters 2 and 3 have been written together to assist you to develop your understanding about human life course development through childhood. Thus, across the two chapters you have studied physical, cognitive, emotional, social and personal development through childhood. This reading has been contextualised within the framework of current national policies, in particular the influential green paper *Every child matters* (DfES, 2003). In this chapter, the focus has been on three of the key outcomes arising from that paper: *enjoying and achieving; making a positive contribution;* and *achieving economic well-being,* which have offered opportunities to explore cognitive and psychological development and the impact of socio-economic issues on child development.

However, in summarising the two chapters, the most significant and fundamental message to impart is that although, for the purposes of this book, I have separated the outcomes to explore the different areas of a child's development, the reality is that the outcomes are interdependent (DfES, 2004, page 8). Hence, in order to take an holistic approach to understanding life course development in childhood, it is necessary to consider each of the aspects addressed in these two chapters. Realistically, then, in order to understand a child's development and the influences upon it, you need to explore a range of complex human behaviours, situations and experiences. This cannot be achieved by the social work practitioner alone. It would need to be the result of integrated, shared information gathering which is, in the most part, influenced by the child themselves, along with their carers and family.

This notion of an holistic, comprehensive approach to understanding development is also integral to the other chapters in this reflective reader. As you study the next chapter about development during adolescence, you will find that your reading and the activities you have undertaken in Chapters 2 and 3, will be relevant and helpful. Whilst the next chapter moves on from the agenda within the *Every child matters* national strategic direction, you will be directed to similar, national policy guidance which is influencing professional practice with adolescents. You will find it interesting to attempt to make the links between Chapters 2 and 3 and the next chapter in order to analyse how young people moving through their lives experience the influence of these policies and professional practice that they might encounter. It is therefore advisable that you keep your notes and work on the activities so that you may refer back to them.

Annotated further reading and research

Aldgate, J, Jones, D, Rose, W and Jeffery, C (2006) *The developing world of the child.* London: Jessica Kingsley.
This contemporary text has, much like this reflective reader, been written to reflect current national initiatives and acknowledged desirable outcomes for children. The text is structured into three parts; the first offering chapters that explore a range of theoretical perspectives on child development; the second part being dedicated to particular age-related phases of childhood; and the final part being related to direct work with children. If you have found Chapters 2 and 3 of this text useful and interesting, you are likely to find Aldgate et al.'s (2006) text is also valuable.

The Who Cares Trust. **www.thewhocarestrust.org.uk**
This is the website of a national charity set up to promote the interests of children and young people who are being cared for by local authorities, for example in foster care or residential homes. In this chapter you have looked at how psychological development may be influenced by respect for children's rights and provision of opportunities to participate and be listened to. The Who Cares Trust and their web-based information is underpinned by these principles and offers links to some informative publications.

Child Poverty Action Group. **www.cpag.org.uk**
CPAG is the leading charity campaigning for the abolition of poverty among children and young people in the UK and for the improvement of the lives of low income families. Their website is easy to 'navigate' and provides access to a range of publications, information and resources, including links to other related sites and key statistical data.

4 Development in adolescence

3.1.5 The nature of social work practice

- The place of theoretical perspectives and evidence from international research in assessment and decision-making processes in social work practice.

3.2.2 Problem solving skills
3.2.2.2 Gathering information
3.2.2.3. Analysis and synthesis
3.2.2.4 Intervention and evaluation

3.2.3. Communication skills

- Listen actively to others, engage appropriately with the life experiences of service users, understand accurately their viewpoint and overcome personal prejudices to respond appropriately to a range of complex personal and interpersonal situations.

3.2.4 Skills in working with others

- Involve users of social work services in ways that increase their resources, capacity and power to influence factors affecting their lives.
- Consult actively with others, including service users, who hold relevant information or expertise.

Introduction

In this chapter you will have the opportunity to explore different approaches to understanding development in adolescence, within the context of contemporary strategic developments aimed to meet the needs of young people. A selection of extracts from, and signposts to, theoretical texts, research and policy documents are provided to enable you to reflect upon the knowledge base and its implications for social work practice. Most readers of this text are likely to have personal experiences of developing in adolescence and therefore your reflections will be influenced by the values and perceptions that you have developed through your own life course. The reflective, interactive activities provided throughout the chapter will help you to identify these and understand the impact of your own experiences on your views of others.

The structure of this chapter has been influenced by the *Youth matters* government green paper which was published in July 2005 (DfES, 2005). *Youth matters* is a consultation document which sets out a strategy which aims to fundamentally reform services for young people. It builds on the principles of *Every child matters* (DfES, 2003), which were discussed in earlier chapters in this book, namely the five key outcomes for young people: being healthy; staying safe; enjoying and achieving; making a positive contribution; and achieving economic well-being. These outcomes represent themes which are integrated into the three sections of this chapter. Each section topic reflects a chapter or chapters of the *Youth matters* document and raises reflective questions which will help you to:

- Evaluate how young people are empowered to have their voice heard and to make choices that impact upon their life course development in adolescence;
- Develop your understanding of how young people develop as citizens through the period known as adolescence;

- Consider some of the perceived complexities and diversities in individual experiences of development through adolescence.

As with all of the chapters in this book, you are encouraged to work through the materials and activities systematically, making notes and recording your reflections and responses as you do so. It is important that you maintain a record of your studies on this chapter, as that record will provide evidence of your continuing professional development and your commitment to best social work practice. Further guidance and advice on different ways in which to record and share your learning are given in Chapter 7 of this book.

As part of this introduction, and before you start to look in some depth at life course development in adolescence, it is important that you consider what is meant by the terms *adolescent* or *adolescence* and *young people*. Firstly *adolescent* is a noun referring to the person deemed to be experiencing the stage or period of life known as *adolescence*. The term *young person* is a broader term which could encompass a wider group of people, including children. Paludi (2002) in her text that examines *Human development in multicultural contexts* states that:

> The word **adolescence** comes from the Latin verb **adolescere**, which translates as 'to grow to maturity' or 'to grow up'. In the life cycle, adolescence is a transitional stage or bridge between childhood and adulthood. The age at which this transition begins, and its duration or length in time, varies from one person to another. (Paludi, 2002, page 132)

The green paper that you will be reading alongside this chapter, *Youth matters* (DfES, 2005) is explicitly focused on individuals aged between 13 and 19 years. The document uses the term *teenagers* throughout, but states that *some of the proposals it contains are also relevant to young people who are slightly older than 19 or younger than 13* (DfES, 2005, page 4).

As you have seen, Paludi (2002, page 132) refers to transition or bridging stage, and indeed, adolescence is commonly associated with the physical transitions to adulthood, beginning with the biological changes expected in puberty. Yet adolescence can also be seen as a period of psychological transition which includes emotional development, identity development, social development and cognitive development. However, the *normative preoccupation with 'transition to adulthood'* (Gillies, 2000, page 211) has been criticised for pervading research, political ideology and academic texts related to adolescence. Gillies (2000) writes that the *transition to adulthood* is more complex than this and is actually just one part of *a wider transition through life*. Through this critique, Gillies (2000) questions some of the potentially taken-for-granted notions we may hold about the validity of adolescence as a particular period of the life course, stating that it is a *historically specific construction of 'young people'* and *has relied on particular representations of change, instability and immaturity*. Gillies then suggests that the way in which the meaning of 'youth' is constructed in our society, through the media, images, and so on, brings with it vulnerability, dangerousness and the need for care and control (ibid., page 223).

At this point in your reading, it would be beneficial to pause and reflect upon your own understanding of the term *adolescence*. Consider the argument put forward by Gillies

(2000) and whether you might agree with her views or perhaps strongly disagree. Either way, you should consider the evidence upon which you are basing your views and the validity of that evidence. It is also appropriate to question the legitimacy of Gillies' theoretical text – to do this you will need to read the whole paper. You should keep this debate about the way in which adolescence is understood in our society in your mind as you study the next section of this chapter, which focuses on the principal of empowerment and enabling young people to have real influence over their experience of this period in their lives.

Empowering young people – supporting choice

In this section you will read about and consider ways in which young people are empowered to have their voice heard and to make choices that impact upon their life course development in adolescence. The reflective questions that you should consider as you read through this section of the chapter are:

- what do young people say about their lives and what they need?
- what do young people say about development in adolescence in our society?
- what does this mean for my practice with adolescents?

Preparing reading

Before you read the extract, read:

- Department for Education and Skills (DfES) (2005) *Youth matters*, Cm 6629. London: Stationery Office. **www.dfes.gov.uk**
  This is the government green paper discussed in the introduction to the chapter. For this section it would be helpful if you could read Chapters 3 and 5. Chapter 3 *Empowering young people: Things to do and places to go* and Chapter 5 *Supporting choices: Information, advice and guidance* provide the contemporary strategic context for the discussion in this section of the chapter.

Selected extracts

Calder, A and Cope, R (2003) *Breaking barriers? Reaching the hardest to reach.* London: The Prince's Trust.

Introduction
The majority of young people in the UK have a bright future with a strong support network of family and friends, an education and a prosperous career path ahead of them. But for many others it is a very different story.

There are more than 600,000 16–24 year olds in the UK who are economically inactive and not in full time education, and a further 579,000 young people who are unemployed. This is coupled with an estimated 10,000 15 year olds who are 'missing' from schools in England and are not accounted for anywhere in the system.

The scope of this research is to identify the aims and aspirations of these disadvantaged young people, living in different parts of Britain, and to understand the barriers that prevent them from achieving their goals.

How the research was conducted

More than 900 14–25 year olds were consulted during the course of this research. The project used quantitative and qualitative methods to explore the aims and aspirations of disadvantaged young people, and the obstacles that hold them back from achieving their aims.

The research covered four categories of disadvantaged young people:

- The unemployed
- Educational under-achievers
- Ex-offenders and serving prisoners
- Those in or leaving care, aged 16–21

A control group of young people who were not from disadvantaged backgrounds was also included to compare and contrast outcomes.

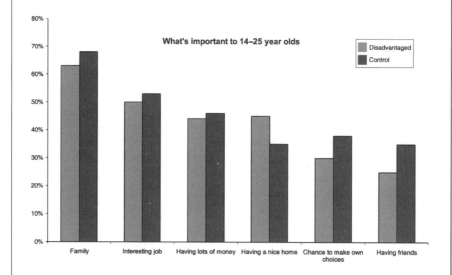

Aspirations by age and gender

Aspiration	Total All	14–17			18–21			22–25		
		Total	Male	Female	Total	Male	Female	Total	Male	Female
Family	63%	58%	59%	57%	70%	71%	67%	65%	65%	65%
Interesting job	51%	58%	57%	58%	46%	43%	51%	39%	47%	26%
Nice home	45%	40%	40%	40%	51%	52%	51%	51%	48%	56%
Having lots of money	43%	43%	53%	29%	41%	43%	38%	45%	44%	46%
Chance to make own choices	30%	32%	25%	43%	30%	25%	36%	22%	24%	19%
Having friends	26%	29%	27%	32%	18%	19%	18%	28%	26%	30%

What holds back disadvantaged 14–25 year olds from achieving their goals

14–17 year old males
- 39 per cent are held back by bad behaviour
- 37 per cent suffer from a lack of confidence

14–17 year old females
- 48 per cent suffer from a lack of confidence
- 28 per cent are held back most by bad behaviour

18–21 year old males
- 51 per cent are held back by a lack of qualifications
- 38 per cent are held back by a criminal record

18–21 year old females
- 47 per cent suffer from a lack of qualifications
- 32 per cent said they don't have enough confidence

22–25 year old males
- 44 per cent are held back by a lack of qualifications
- 38 per cent said that there are not enough suitable jobs or opportunities

22–25 year old females
- 48 per cent said that they don't have enough experience
- 43 per cent are held back by being a parent

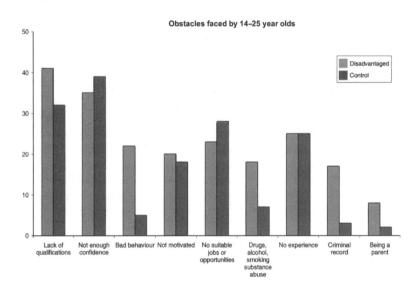

Obstacles faced by 14–25 year olds

Summary
- The aims and aspirations of disadvantaged young people were very similar to the control group. They shift with age and maturity, and are not related to the extent of their social exclusions.
- Young people from disadvantaged backgrounds had very clear perceptions of the barriers that prevented them from achieving their goals.
- Only five per cent of disadvantaged young people said that nothing held them back compared with 13 per cent of those in the control sample.
- Forty-one per cent of the disadvantaged sample considered that they were held back by a lack of qualifications.
- Disadvantaged groups were more likely than the control sample to cite barriers such as disruptive behaviour, a criminal record and drug or alcohol abuse. By their own admission, these barriers were likely to occur as a result of their own bad behaviour.

- Forty-five per cent of the disadvantaged group who were held back by drugs or alcohol abuse were also held back by a criminal record.
- There was a significant difference in attitude to parenthood between males and females. Males did not consider that parenthood holds them back. However, 43 per cent of 22–25 year old females said that being a parent is a barrier.
- Disadvantaged young people valued the ability to make informed choices for themselves.
- Young people, irrespective of their background, considered a lack of confidence as one of their biggest obstacles.
- Those aged 14–17 placed a greater emphasis on work and material achievements, while those aged 18–25 focused on relationships and self-fulfilment.
- Family was central to many disadvantaged young people. Thirty-one per cent said that having a family was their top priority for the future. Eighty-two per cent cited either family or having a nice home as one of their most important aspirations.

Analysis

The above is a selection of extracts from a research report that was published prior to the *Youth matters* green paper. The report is the culmination of a three-year partnership project, developed by the Prince's Trust, to examine the aims and aspirations of 14–25 year-old people and to look at what they perceive as being the barriers to meeting their goals in life. This gives you a little of the context of this research and the report. As you reflect upon, and critically analyse, any research, it is advisable to start by understanding its context. For example, as we have done here, looking at when it was undertaken, by whom and for what purpose. Further advice on critical analysis of research and knowledge evidence is provided in the final chapter of this book.

You should also note that I have provided only selected extracts that I have considered to be relevant to this chapter and section of this book. I would strongly recommend that you access the full report and then draw out the most significant elements to meet your own learning and practice development needs. For instance, you will see that in the extract there is only limited information about the research methodology and the participant sample. This is due to restrictions of space here, but, in the full report, there is much more detail about the sample composition and the data collection processes undertaken in this research.

Research of this type is one way in which young people are empowered to have their voice heard and identify and clarify their ideas and concerns. However, research involving children and young people *raises interesting methodological and ethical issues* (Morrow and Richards, 1996, page 105). In particular, researchers must ensure ethical practices in the research processes of data collection, analysis and interpretation, dissemination and protection of research participants. However, as concluded by Morrow and Richards (ibid.) *to avoid asking the questions because they are ethically difficult, thereby excluding children from research, is an ethical position in itself.*

Over 900 young people participated in Calder and Cope's research (2003). The authors state that *the best way to acknowledge the participation of these young people is to listen to what they think about their lives and recognise that they know what is best for them*

(Calder and Cope, 2003, page 2). The key issues that participants raised as being important to them are indicated in the first graph within the extract. It can be seen that
having a family of their own appears to be the most important aspiration that these
young people expressed. However, as Calder and Cope note in their report, (2003, page
7) and as shown in the table of 'Aspirations by age and gender', the participants' *perception (and definition) of family was dependent upon their age, gender and personal
circumstances.* So for the younger participants, aged between 14 and 17 years, family
meant parents and siblings, whilst for the older group, aged between 18 and 25, family
related to their own household with children and partner. It is interesting to reflect
upon this finding and what the expressed aspirations of these young people tell us
about their life course development. The impact of this finding on our understanding
of human development in adolescence could be explored from a range of theoretical
perspectives: biological perspectives focusing on physical development and needs;
sociological perspectives focusing on environmental, social influences, expectations
and norms; or psychological theories focusing on cognitive and behavioural development. These perspectives are explained in more depth in Crawford and Walker (2003).
The graph and related table in the extract also present data in respect of other issues
that are important to young people. As you study the data, attempt to deconstruct
and question, or look beneath the figures, as we have done in exploring the first data
set, above. Additionally, you should consider what the similarities and differences
between the *disadvantaged* group and the control group may indicate. I have also
included extracted data, in tabular and graph formats, that indicates young people's
perceptions of the barriers that prevented them from achieving their goals. Again,
you are invited to explore, interrogate and analyse this data in a similar way.

Another stage in your analysis of this research extract could be to evaluate its relationship to chapters 3 and 5 of the *Youth matters* green paper, suggested as pre-reading
for this section. As you do this, you should consider what this information and knowledge can tell us about developing social work practice. Chapter 3 has *Empowering
young people* in its title and Chapter 5 has *Supporting choices* as the start of its title.
These are significant and relevant words for the discussion in this section of the chapter.
The Department for Education and Skills' (DfES) statement in the foreword to the
green paper, that some young people are disadvantaged in terms of accessing opportunities, is borne out in the research summary findings, given in the extract above.
Additionally, in Chapter 3 of *Youth matters* (DfES, 2005) there is evidence that some
of the views of young people, as expressed in the *Breaking barriers?: Reaching the
hardest to reach* (Calder and Cope, 2003) investigation, are being addressed (DfES,
2005, page 37). You might consider, however, that direct comparison between these
two information sources is not possible, as the two documents have very different
purposes and hail from very different organisations. The research analyses views and
life course ambitions of a particular sample group of young people whilst the green
paper focuses on strategic service change at a national, structural level. Yet, I would
argue that there should be evidence of the former impacting upon the latter, and that
therefore, linkages and integration should be evident.

Another aspect of your critique might be that in looking at the issues that have been
raised by over 900 research participants, and a seemingly all-encompassing strategy
document, individual needs and biographical life course development is omitted.

Indeed a theme that you will have detected throughout this book, is the importance of the individual narrative and the distinctive life course experiences of each person. This issue of the tension between the social construction of self (which may be related to any framework, for example age-related as in *teenager* or *adult*) and the individual self, is discussed by Hockey and James (2003, page 202) in their exploration of *Social identities across the life course*. Hockey and James explain that individual identity and collective, shared identities are integrated and mutually dependent. In other words, the two are intrinsically related, each being influenced by the other. Hence, our individual life course experiences would have no context or framework, without us, as individuals, being able to construct and validate those experiences within the collective social identity.

In the concluding section of the research report from which the extracts above have been taken, the authors note that being able to make their own choices is highly important to young people:

> They want to be provided with sufficient information to make their own decisions and resent being told what is best for them. At each life stage they encounter a system that directs rather than engages.

> Social support services need to provide a range of suitable options, depending on circumstance, but leave the final decision to the individual. However, often the nature of the support on offer is inextricably linked to the benefit structure, greatly limiting the options available.

> (Calder and Cope, 2003, page 14)

Personal reflections

The pre-reading, the extract and related analysis above have focused on exploring what young people say about development in adolescence in our society and the ways in which they can be empowered to take control and make choices during their development as adolescents. Reflect on your reading of the chapter so far and imagine that you want to find out about young people's perceptions of the experience of developing as an adolescent in our society today. Attempt to frame your thoughts as a small number of potential questions and then write them up as if you were developing a questionnaire to be used to enable young people to express their views, wishes, perceptions and feelings. Note down the questions you have formulated, then also write a few sentences with each question to indicate what you would be trying to find out by asking that question.

Comment

Writing questionnaires is more difficult than you might at first think (Bell, 1999, page 118). However, a very straightforward starting point for this activity might be to ask young people themselves what it is that they think you need to understand and know, if you are to appreciate their needs and experiences. A small group of young people could help to devise and/or pilot your questionnaire. The website for YoungMinds Magazine (**www.youngminds.org.uk**), a national charity that aims to improve the mental health of children and young people, provides ideas on different formats of questionnaires and discussion about the ways in which consultation with young people has influenced their questionnaire design. Additionally, the green paper, *Youth matters* (DfES, 2005, pages 75–7) is itself a consultation document and as such includes a number of consultation questions. You may find it interesting to read through these questions and consider whether you feel they provide an effective and appropriate consultation mechanism.

Practical implications and activities

As you have been developing your thinking about the sorts of questions that might be appropriate to ask of young people in order to gain a better understanding of their experiences and views, you may have thought about the strengths and weaknesses of using written questions, through questionnaires, as a way of engaging with young people. Questionnaires, are only one way in which to enable young people to express their views and experiences of adolescence. Think about the practicalities of working with young people and the ways in which they might be empowered to exercise choice and to participate meaningfully. Draw a table like this one below, and write in other examples of activities that you could implement in order to empower young people and increase their opportunities to have their views heard. An example is given below to get you started.

Examples of methods of enabling participation and empowerment	What are the practical implications of implementing this activity?	What skills would I need to develop in order to be effective in implementing this activity
Written questionnaires	– Can be expensive – Can be time-consuming – Might be misinterpreted by those completing them – Will enable me to access a large number of young people – Will allow me to gather a great deal of information	Skills in developing effective questionnaires Skills in data analysis

Developing as citizens – making a contribution

In this section of the chapter you will have the opportunity to further your understanding of how young people develop as citizens through the period known as adolescence. The reflective questions that you should consider as you read through this section of the chapter are:

- how do young people develop through adolescence into adulthood?
- how have my experiences of adolescence influenced my values and my understanding of life course development through this period of life?
- how do I develop my practice to enable young people to develop?

Preparatory reading

Before you read the extract, read:

- Department for Education and Skills (DfES) (2005) *Youth matters*, Cm 6629. London: Stationery Office. **www.dfes.gov.uk**
  For this section it would be helpful if you could read Chapter 4 *Young people as citizens: Making a contribution.*

- Russell, I M (2005) *A national framework for youth action and engagement.* Norwich: HMSO.
  This document is the executive summary report to The Russell Commission.

- Department of Health (DoH) (2004) *National service framework for children, young people and maternity services.* London: Stationery Office.
  It would be useful to familiarise yourself with Standard 4: *All young people have access to age-appropriate services which are responsive to their specific needs as they grow into adulthood.*

These three documents provide the contemporary strategic context for the discussion in this section of the chapter.

Extract

Jones, G (2002) *The youth divide: diverging paths to adulthood.* York: Joseph Rowntree Foundation. **www.jrf.org.uk**

Extension of youth

'Youth' is a social construction, and the way it is understood as a concept varies across cultures and over time. Since youth first emerged as a 'stage in life' in its modern form it has been continually extended, largely as a result of government policies. Where a few decades ago it may have been possible to think about a single ordered sequence of transitions from childhood to adulthood, the extension of education and training in particular has driven a wedge between the two, highlighting and extending the process of youth, but also making it far more complex (Jones, 1997).

As a working definition let us think of childhood as a period of economic dependence (on parents or other carers) and adulthood as the achievement of economic independence, though these are simplifications (as this report will show). Youth is thus somewhere between the two (Table 1), a period of semi-dependence during which transition to adult independence occurs (Jones and Wallace, 1992). This period of youth has become extended, and the transitions to adulthood have become more complex. The experience of young people growing up nowadays is likely to be very different from the kind of youth experienced by their parents.

Table 1 Extended transitions to adulthood

Childhood	Youth	Adulthood
School	College or training scheme	Labour market
Parental home	Intermediate household, living with peers or alone	Independent home

Child in family	Intermediate statuses, inc. single parenthood, cohabiting partner	Partner–parent
More secure housing	Transitional housing in youth housing market (e.g. furnished flats and bedsits)	More secure housing
'Pocket money' income	'Component' or partial income (e.g. transitional NMW)	Full adult income
Economic 'dependence'	Economic semi-dependence	Economic 'independence'

Polarisation

The analysis of large national data sets makes it possible to see the extent to which new divisions are occurring in young people's experiences. Using data from two national birth cohort studies (of young people born 12 years apart), Bynner and his colleagues (2002, forthcoming) mapped the changes in patterns of transition to adulthood.

Key changes in the transition to adulthood

- The transition to adulthood can be broken down into different but *interconnected strands* or pathways (Table 1). Young people can become adult according to one criterion not but another. Thus they can become economically independent but still live in the parental home, or live independently but still with parental support.

- There is therefore *no longer a normative ordering* along a single pathway (comprising a school-to-work transition followed some years later by a household-and-family-formation transition). This kind of pathway was perhaps uniquely prevalent in the 1950s and the early 1960s.

- 'Progress' to adult independence may involve *backtracking* (including drop-out from education or training, returns to the parental home, and tentative partnership formation and cohabitation).

- There are now more likely to be *intermediate stages* between leaving school and entry into the labour market, between living in the parental home and having a home of one's own, and (perhaps) between being a child in a family and being a parent or partner in one. Each of these stages is, however, potentially problematic.

- The *significance of individual events* (rites of passage perhaps) within these transitions has changed. Since household formation has become more separated from family formation transitions, leaving home has become a more important life event in itself. Similarly, leaving school becomes less significant when it is not accompanied by starting employment.

- The end product, *adult citizenship, is less secure* and less clearly defined: access to the labour market, an independent home and a stable family life is more in doubt than before. Though young people still aspire to conventional constructions of adulthood, we should beware of seeming to judge them on outdated criteria of 'success' and 'failure'.

- Perhaps one of the main changes in recent decades has been that *young people are seeking more independence*. This dynamic is likely to continue despite the lack of supporting structures, with or without state support, and with or without family support. Thus, many young people leave home without resources and despite the risk of homelessness, because they need to become independent of their parents.

- At the same time, however, the period of dependent youth has been extended. The extension of the period of dependent youth raises the question of *whom they should be dependent on*. Responsibility is being transferred from the state onto parents precisely at a time when there is increased likelihood of marital breakdown, and an increased chance that young people will not be living with their two natural parents.

- A *holistic approach* is needed to understand youth transitions. Social trends and policy interventions that affect one area of young people's lives are likely to affect other areas as well.

The ways in which this transition happens vary between social groups. Typically and historically, middle-class transitions have been more protracted than working-class ones, and middle-class families have provided economic support for longer. Women have similarly entered partnerships and become parents earlier than men (Jones, 1988). Social class and gender differences such as these may be changing, but they are not disappearing, as the report will show.

Social exclusion in youth

How do these changes in transitions to adulthood affect social exclusion and inclusion?

The relationship between the child and the wider society (citizenship) is to a great extent, and for better or worse, mediated by parents or other carers (thus, for example, welfare benefits are paid to parents rather than to children, and child poverty is measured at the level of a child's household rather than that of the individual child). Young people are possibly in an even more anomalous social position, half citizen in their own right and half citizen-by-proxy, via their parents or carers. Thus, inequalities (and advantage or disadvantage, integration and exclusion) accrue to young people in part directly as individuals, and in part indirectly via their parents. Individual characteristics may not therefore provide adequate indicators of social disadvantage and exclusion in youth: family characteristics may also need to be taken into account.

Social exclusion is generally identified where individuals are excluded from employment, housing, health care, etc. However, all young people are to some extent excluded from aspects of the wider (adult) society. They are marginalised as an age group. But young people are also a heterogeneous group, and people who are of the same age may be at different stages in their transitions to adulthood, and suffer social exclusion in different forms and to different degrees. Being 'in transition', some may not yet be seeking employment and housing, or they may not yet be taking responsibility for their own health care; others, however, may have sought these but failed to gain access to them. This creates a further set of problems for researchers seeking indicators of social exclusion.

Part of any programme of research on social exclusion in youth will concern itself with currently excluded groups: these will be the most visible, and probably also those who are identified as social problems (often meaning the problems for society, rather than the problems of society for young people). Young people who are identified as excluded and in need of support are only the tip of the iceberg, but it is they who are targeted for positive or negative intervention. These may include homeless and jobless young people and teenage parents; they may include young people who have turned to drugs, alcohol or crime. Because many dimensions of inequality may be cross-cutting, we find that many in these groups are disadvantaged by social class, gender, ethnicity and disability. In targeting the most easily identified groups, we should be careful not to close our minds to those who may be excluded or at the margins of society (perhaps even for the same reasons) but are less visible and pose fewer problems for society. Research on young people might indicate new forms and causes of social exclusion and identify hitherto unknown vulnerable groups.

Analysis

The extract above is taken from the introductory chapter of a Joseph Rowntree Foundation (JRF) report based on a number of research projects undertaken within the Young People programme; the Action in Rural Areas programme; and the Work and Opportunity programme (Jones, 2002). In the preface to the report, Jones states that:

> The overwhelming finding from the studies cited is that, far from being a homogenous group ('youth'), young people are becoming more and more sharply divided, between those who have and those who have not ... We see polarisation of experience in every aspect of transition to adulthood – a 'Youth Divide'. (Jones, 2002, page vi)

One of the first things that you might identify is a common assertion between this quotation, the extract given above, some of the discussion in the earlier section and Gillies (2000) argument put forward in the introduction to this chapter – namely the assertion that any understanding formed about the life course period of *adolescence* or *youth* is historically, socially and culturally specific. Thus, whether you are trying to understand how an individual young person is developing through their adolescence, or to characterise the experience of adolescence at a more structural level, you cannot do so without reference to the *changes and continuities* evident within the life course. Hunt (2005) explains that *continuity is evident in that youth remains a significant and relatively 'separate' phase of life* and that *change is observable in the growing commodification of youth culture which is itself becoming increasingly fragmented* (2005, page 103). Examples of the types of changes that Hunt refers to, particularly in respect of the transition to adulthood, are also evident in the extract, particularly in Table 1. The table is based upon research undertaken to explore how young people's lives changed over a period of twenty years (Bynner et al., 2002). Bynner et al.'s main findings reflect a range of notable differences in development though adolescence as experienced by the two research participant cohorts, for example, changes in employment practices, financial status, educational opportunities, family and partner relationships, social inclusion and psychological health. The diagram below, Figure 4.1, illustrates a range of potential influences and changes over time, from both a social and an individual level, which may have a bearing upon how young people experience and develop through this period of their lives.

As you will note, in the extract Jones (2002) considers *how these changes in transitions to adulthood affect social exclusion and inclusion*. Given the discussion above, you might ask why this question is not reversed to read *how social exclusion and inclusion affect the transition to adulthood* and the experience of adolescence. In the pre-reading for this section, you will have seen how the National Service Framework (NSF) (DoH, 2004) Standard 4, sets standards to improve life chance opportunities, plan for

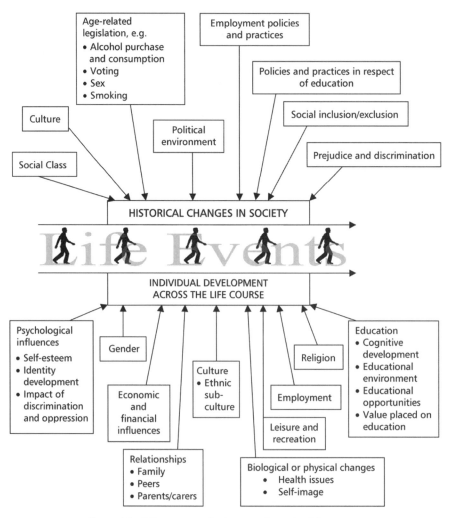

Figure 4.I – Influences on the journey through adolescence

transitions to living independently and assist educational and career development. The report to the Russell Commission (Russell, 2005, page 4), also recommended as pre-reading for this section, refers to *youth action and engagement* and focuses on youth volunteering so that young people may have a *menu of opportunity* and will thus *find meaningful ways of contributing to their communities.* Similarly, the green paper, *Youth matters,* that you have been referred to throughout this chapter, could be seen to have an overarching focus on addressing issues of social exclusion for young people, with Chapter 4 (the pre-reading suggested for this section of the chapter) focusing on *active citizenship approaches* and *opportunities.* Chapter 4 of the green paper suggests a two-way relationship between young people and society, which draws attention to *rights and responsibilities* (DfES, 2005). However, in the full research report from which the extract has been taken, Jones (2005, page 37), critiques the policy framework that only confers rights on young people once they have learned social responsibilities. This is reflected in the green paper *Youth matters* and in the Russell Commission, where volunteering is seen as *a route back to learning, jobs and society more generally* (DfEs, 2005, page 40; Russell, 2005). Jones suggests that from the perspective of young people themselves this may need to be the other way around, in other words, involving and contributing to society may need to come after rights.

You can detect common themes emerging in relation to how people develop through and experience adolescence. Hunt (2005, page 121), referring to a report entitled *The burden of youth*, draws attention to the contemporary policy framework and social constructions of adolescence as *putting teenagers under considerable pressure* to take up opportunities, to succeed both in education and employment and to have high expectations. You may also be aware of the national Connexions service which is a partnership service that aims to provide advice and support to young people aged between 13 and 19 years. You may have noted that the *Youth matters* green paper includes provision for the *Connexions Card* which is freely available to young people and rewards them for learning, work-based training and voluntary activities (**www.connexions-direct.com**). It can be seen, therefore, how this scheme fits within the overall policy framework and contributes to perceived social expectations.

Success in education, employment and voluntary activities may seem laudable principles, but as you have seen in the extracts and readings so far in this chapter, many young people experience inequalities and exclusion through their adolescence, and we should reflect upon how the social construction of adolescence and the high expectations referred to, impact upon their experiences and development through this stage of life. Jones (2002, page vi) coined the phrase a 'youth divide' and concludes her report by stating:

> Inequalities persist among young people and in some respects they have deepened. However, the polarisation described in this report hides a more complex and disturbing picture. In the social hierarchy of young people, between the 'socially included' and the 'socially excluded', there is a large (and largely invisible) group trying to survive on scarce resources, including their own resilience. (Jones, 2005, page 44)

Personal reflections

Refer back to the diagram given in Figure 4.1 *Influences on the journey through adolescence*. Think about your own experience of adolescence, and imagine yourself progressing along the pathway or journey depicted in the illustration. Then look at each of the potential influences shown and, using each influence as a heading, reflect upon and note down the way in which that particular facet of life may have impacted upon your own life course development through adolescence.

Can you identify very specific examples under those topics that are relevant? For example, when considering *policies and practices in respect of education* at the structural level and how they may have impacted upon my experience of adolescence, I can reflect upon my experience of secondary education and moving to a large school which was in the process of changing its admission criteria to become a comprehensive school, following the national demise of entry examinations at the age of 11 years. This impacted greatly upon my experience of education at that time and the peers and friends that I had access to.

To conclude, write a few reflective sentences that draw together your learning from this exercise, addressing the reflective question – *how have my experiences of adolescence influenced my values and my understanding of life course development through this period of life?* As a further extension of this activity, you could also compare your reflections on your own adolescent experience with the contemporary policy outlined in the *Youth matters* strategy. So, for example, how did you develop as a citizen? Did you make a positive contribution to society during your adolescent years? Did you, for example, take up volunteering and if so, did this make a difference to your experiences?

Given the discussion in this section of the chapter, in respect of historical changes to the experience and construction of adolescence, try to carry out the same exercise for someone that you know who is in another generation – perhaps an older or younger relative, depending upon your own age, of course! Do you think that these influences impacted differently for them?

Comment

You may have found this exercise quite complex, as human life is not as straightforward as an illustration made up of lines and boxes! You may have been reminded, as you thought through the various influences, about Hockey and James' (2003, page 202) work on *Social identities across the life course* that you read about earlier in the chapter. Their view that developing identities are influenced by an integrated mix of the shared, social and the individual, personal context is replicated in the links between the structural, the historical and the personal influences shown in the diagram. Indeed, using the example from my own life course, discussed above, the structural educational policy changes had a direct bearing upon my personal experiences.

The next activity encourages you to think through your own developing practice and the practical implications of your learning. As you work on this, you should be mindful of your learning from this exercise and be explicit about how your own experiences impact upon your values. *Your own personal values will . . . inevitably influence how you do your job and the decisions and choices that you make. For this reason it is important to be as aware as possible of what those values are and where they come from* (Beckett and Maynard, 2005, page 14).

Practical implications and activities

The *Youth matters* green paper, which is both a consultative and a strategic document, outlines the government's proposals to meet the needs of young people in contemporary society. The proposals include:

- making services more flexible, integrated, efficient and effective, to respond to what young people, their parents and carers want;
- balancing greater opportunities and support with the promotion of responsibilities;
- improving outcomes for all young people, including narrowing the gap between those who do well and those who do less well;

- increasing choice through the involvement of a wide range of organisations in service provision.

Imagine that you are responsible for practice development in an organisation that provides support services for young people. Given the policy direction indicated in the green paper and the knowledge gained from research, make a list of achievable, practical changes in practice that could be implemented to improve the services that support young people developing into adulthood. To get you started, here are just two possible examples.

- Developing information, advice and guidance services that are accessible to all young people; in different languages and different formats.
- Mapping current service provision across agencies in the locality to identify duplication and gaps in service provision.

Developing through a complex and troubled adolescence

The summary of Chapter 6 of the *Youth matters* green paper starts with the sentence *Young people at risk often lead complicated and troubled lives* (DfES, 2005, page 55). In this final section of this chapter you will explore why some young people are considered to be at risk of experiencing development through adolescence as complex and troubled. You will also examine a predictive approach to identifying potential risk so that it might be proactively prevented through co-ordinated engagement with young people themselves and those around them, communities and society.

The reflective questions that you should consider when learning about theories and models of practice generally, particularly as you read through this section of the chapter, are:

- why do some young people experience adolescence as complex and troubled periods of their lives?
- why is this knowledge relevant to improving and developing social work practice?
- why might this challenge stereotypes and assumptions, or taken-for-granted approaches?

Preparatory reading

Before you read this extract, read:

- Department for Education and Skills (DfES) (2005) *Youth matters*, Cm 6629. London: Stationery Office. **www.dfes.gov.uk**
  This is the government green paper discussed in the introduction to the chapter. For this section it would be helpful if you could read Chapter 6 *All young people achieving: Reforming targeted support* which provides the contemporary strategic context for the discussion in this section of the chapter.
- National Assembly for Wales, Department for Training and Education (2000) *Extending Entitlement: Supporting young people in Wales*. Cardiff: Welsh Assembly Government. **www.wales.gov.uk/youngpeople**
  You will find this whole report of relevance and interest in respect to your studies of life

course development in adolescence. It is particularly relevant to this section of the chapter, as it sets out the principles and priorities for promoting opportunity and choice for all young people in Wales aged between 11 and 25 years, and the extract below evaluates a multi-agency service in Swansea, Wales. It will, of course, be more generally pertinent if you are working in, or studying, social work in Wales. The document has 10 chapters, but the first two chapters provide an overall summary of the key messages, recommendations and policy focus. Additionally, since its publication in 2000, there have been supplementary direction and guidance documents, which I recommend that you access. In particular, Haines and Case (2004) who are also the authors of the journal article accessed for the extract below, report on the findings of a pilot study to establish baseline measurements from which to evaluate the effectiveness of the implementation of *Extending entitlement.*

Extract

Case, S, and Haines, K (2004) Promoting Prevention: Evaluating a Multi-agency Initiative of Youth Consultation and Crime Prevention in Swansea. *Children and Society*, 18 (5), 355–70

Promoting Prevention is a cross-cutting multi-agency partnership in Swansea involving the statutory and voluntary sectors, with the central aim of preventing youth offending amongst 10 to 17 year olds. Promoting Prevention is based on the principles of educational and economic inclusion, and forms Swansea's response to the requirements of the Crime and Disorder Act 1998. The initiative aims to implement Strategic Priority 5 of the 'Safer Swansea' Crime and Disorder Reduction Plan, specifically:

- prevention of offending
- prevention of re-offending by first-time offenders and persistent young offenders

The Promoting Prevention partnership developed from within the Youth Offending Team (YOT) Working Group and was intended to unify the primary duty under the Crime and Disorder Act to prevent youth offending with the objective of the YOT Steering Group to promote a socially inclusive approach to youth crime. For Swansea YOT, involvement in primary prevention was seen as essential. The Promoting Prevention plan was established by the YOT and Community Safety Department as a key vehicle for primary prevention and for focusing the activity of the Safer Swansea Crime Reduction Plan.

A task and finish group involving the agency partners was established to set out principles and objectives. The objective was to establish wide ownership and participation in a youth crime reduction strategy that established universal rights for young people in Swansea and delivered targeted services to those in need. Thus, 'Promoting Prevention' is the umbrella term for the youth crime prevention initiatives of the City and County of Swansea.

Local programmes of youth crime prevention in Swansea are theoretically underpinned by the *Risk Factor Prevention Paradigm*, which identifies risk factors for offending in the key domains of the young person's life (for example, family, school, neighbourhood, peers) and implements preventative measures designed to counteract them, as well as identifying and enhancing protective factors (see Hawkins and Catalano, 1992). The most beneficial risk and protective factor-focused schemes thus far have addressed multiple risk factors and offered multiple outcomes (Hawkins and Catalano, 1992). However, the bulk of the cogent evidence comes from North America (for example, Sherman and others, 1998), thus limiting generalisability due to socio-cultural differences such as firearm laws, ethnic composition, gang culture and widespread drug use (see Goldblatt and Lewis,1998). Although many promising approaches exist in the UK, they are yet to be rigorously evaluated (for example, Utting, 1996). Little is known about optimal intervention strategies with young people, particularly the relative efficacy of targeting whole populations (that is universal services) as opposed to individuals (for example, children at risk or known offenders). Also, evidence is needed to indicate the most effective points to intervene in the developmental pathway leading to offending and/or in criminal careers (Vassallo and others, 2002).

The evaluation assesses the effect of the Promoting Prevention initiative on youth offending behaviour in Swansea by identifying changes in self-reported levels of risk and protective factors for offending, as well as self-reported drug use and self-reported offending. Understanding the causes of and explanations for youth offending in Swansea is important because this will ultimately enable agencies contributing to Promoting Prevention to more effectively target their resources and interventions, whilst initiating new services in response to need and gaps in provision as identified by service users (that is young people).

Promoting Prevention is driven by the principles of consultation and empowerment that have underpinned the local authority's approach to youth service provision since the inception of the Promoting Positive Behaviour (PPB) initiative (1996) and the first annual Swansea Youth Conference (1999). Therefore, the City and County of Swansea operated to a youth inclusion and enfranchisement agenda prior to the Welsh Assembly Government's articulation of this ethos in recent policy. It encourages a positive and optimistic view of children as having the right to be consulted about all issues that affect them (following Article 12 of the United Nations (UN) Convention on the Rights of the Child 1989). Local service providers are encouraged to hear the voices of children and young people, especially those of potentially disadvantaged children (for example, with special needs, from other cultures, in public care), listen to their views, and ensure that services respond to their needs and aspirations (see also National Assembly for Wales, 2000). Provision and policy are structured around entitlement to a range of services designed to promote young people's attainment and development as individuals (see also National Assembly Policy Unit, 2002).

Promoting Prevention services

Promoting Prevention embodies a range of corporate and strategic interventions addressing factors known to place young people at risk of offending (for example, school exclusion, truancy and pupil disaffection, lack of training and employment opportunities, drug and alcohol misuse, social exclusion), as well as a range of interventions based in equal measure on restorative justice and social inclusion. It incorporates a number of important elements.

Analysis

This extract is taken from a journal article which provides an account of the evaluation of a multi-agency, multiple intervention initiative to prevent youth offending in Swansea. This is clearly about a particular service with a particular approach, the findings of which, the authors acknowledge, *may not be globally-applicable as influential factors may be dependent upon social, cultural, economic, legal and criminal justice processes in a particular country, city or even neighbourhood* (Case and Haines, 2004, page 367). That being said, this work does substantially add to the developing knowledge base of best practice and what works in supporting young people through this period of their lives. This evaluative study adds to our understanding of why some young people experience adolescence as a complex and troubled period of their lives, and uses explicit theoretical underpinnings to develop improving support practices. As Hood (2004, page viii) states *the more we understand these problems the more capable we shall be to respond to them with justice, humanity and rationally based argument.*

There are two main specific elements of the extract that you might question, critique and consider worthy of additional enquiry: firstly, the links to other strategies, research and reading that you have undertaken in this chapter; and secondly, the underpinning philosophy and theoretical basis to the approach outlined.

With respect to the correlations between this initiative and relevant policy, strategy and research papers, you could start by underlining some of the key words in the extract, for example: *rights for young people; consultation; empowerment; disadvantage; promote attainment and development;* and *social inclusion.* These are just some of the concepts addressed in this short extract which provide an indication of the philosophy of the project. Throughout this chapter, within the *Extending entitlement* Welsh strategy document, the green paper *Youth matters* and the research extracts, the significance of recognising the rights and responsibilities of young people within a supportive structure of empowerment and engagement, in order to make a difference to young people's development through adolescence, has been highlighted. In their abstract preceding the journal article, Case and Haines (2004: 355) confirm that *evaluation indicates that Promoting Prevention's consultative methodology is an empowering and engaging way of targeting interventions to promote positive behaviours and prevent anti-social behaviour in young people* and *it is thus underpinned by universal principles of youth consultation and empowerment* (ibid., page 359).

In Chapter 6 of the *Youth matters* green paper *All young people achieving: Reforming targeted support* you will have noticed the emphasis on *targeted support* from *integrated services*, along with *a focus on prevention and early intervention.* Bearing in mind that the green paper was published in 2005, sometime after the *cross-cutting multi-agency partnership in Swansea* was evaluated, it appears as though the evidence of best practice may be being used to inform strategic policy directions. In fact, the Promoting Prevention initiative has been proclaimed as an example of best practice with young people by the Policy Unit for the National Assembly for Wales **www.wales.gov.uk**. Additionally, Case and Haines (2004, page 368) conclude their article by stressing the importance of creating a *local climate of change that values the ideas of 'community'* *and 'citizenship'.* The notion of *citizenship* is embedded in the *Youth matters* strategy and has been discussed earlier in this chapter. Similarly the word *community* appears no less than 68 times in the green paper, most commonly related to community sector service provision or youth involvement in communities.

The second element of the extract that I suggested you could explore further was the underpinning philosophy and theoretical basis to the approach outlined. The authors make this explicit in the extract by stating that *local programmes ... are theoretically underpinned by the* Risk Factor Prevention Paradigm (RFPP). They go on to explain briefly what this means and to refer to the work of Hawkins and Catalano (1992). Dr J David Hawkins and Dr Richard F Catalano are American researchers who have, for many years, explored factors that contribute to, or protect against, a child developing problem behaviours. As stated in the extract, Hawkins and Catalano suggested multiple *risk factors* and *protective factors* within certain important areas of a young person's life, known as domains. These factors are reproduced in the table below.

	Individual/Peer	**Family**	**School**	**Community**
Risk Factors	• Alienation and rebelliousness • Friends who engage in problem behaviour • Favourable attitudes towards problem behaviours • Early initiation of the problem behaviour	• Family history of high-risk behaviour • Family management problems • Family conflict • Parental attitudes and involvement in the problem behaviour	• Early and persistent antisocial behaviour • Academic failure beginning in primary school • Low commitment to school	• Availability of drugs • Community laws and norms favourable toward drug use • Transition and mobility • Low neighbourhood attachment and community disorganisation • Extreme economic and social deprivation
Protective Factors	• Bonding to peers with healthy beliefs and clear standards • Meaningful opportunities to contribute to peer group • Skills to successfully take advantage of opportunities • Recognition of efforts	• Bonding to a family with healthy beliefs and clear standards • Meaningful opportunities to contribute to the family • Skills to successfully take advantage of opportunities • Recognition of efforts	• Bonding to a school that promotes healthy beliefs and clear standards • Meaningful opportunities to contribute to school community • Skills to successfully take advantage of opportunities • Recognition of efforts	• Bonding to a community that promotes healthy beliefs and clear standards • Meaningful opportunities to contribute to the community • Skills to successfully take advantage of opportunities • Recognition of efforts

Adapted from Hawkins and Catalano (1992)

Figure 4.2 – Risk and protective factors

Hawkins and Catalano suggest that, to prevent the problem developing, it is necessary to take a predictive approach. According to their theory, strategies that increase the protective factors, whilst reducing the risk factors, will result in prevention. As you look at the risk and protective factors identified by Hawkins and Catalano in the table above, you may recognise some of these issues as being addressed within the strategic policy documents you have been reading in the chapter. This is just one approach or theory that can be used to explain why some young people may be at risk of experiencing a complex and troubled adolescence. It would be beneficial as part of your learning for you to explore further, not only the similarities between this approach and other risk assessment and management approaches, but also other theories that attempt to explain the different developmental pathways that young people may experience.

Personal reflections

This activity encourages you to refer back to the table above and the risk and protective factors identified by Hawkins and Catalano (1992) and reflect upon why this approach might challenge stereotypes and assumptions, or taken-for-granted ideas about young people moving through the adolescent period of their lives.

Firstly cut out and keep any newspaper, magazine or periodical extracts that report on perceived negative behaviours of young people. Then, using those articles, make a list of some of the phrases and terminology that the media use to describe what is going on. Finally, put that list against Hawkins and Catalano's factors and note where there are similarities. What does this tell you about how the behaviours of young people are constructed in our society?

Comment

My search of newspaper articles, as I write this chapter, provides evidence of a contemporary rhetoric about parents not taking enough responsibility for their children's behaviours, a concern about bullying and violence, alarm about the perceived growth of drug misuse amongst young people, and a need for tougher punishments for unruly behaviour. You may have found similar, additional or very different trends as, like all social phenomenon, these issues are historically and culturally specific. However, when put against the identified risk and protective factors, which you will recall hail from the early 1990s in America, you may find some comparative areas. For example, from my search, I can recognise similarities in the importance given to parental attitudes and the concern about the risks of drug misuse. Given these thoughts and reflections, do you feel that the model offered by Hawkins and Catalano reinforces social constructions of young people's behaviours and stereotypes, or does it assist in challenging some of these views?

Practical implications and activities

At the beginning of this section of the chapter I asked you to keep in mind the reflective question – Why is this knowledge relevant to improving and developing social work practice? This activity will be particularly relevant in helping you to address that question. In the extract, Case and Haines (2004, page 356) raise the issue that there is insufficient evidence about the effectiveness of differently targeted intervention strategies, particularly whether it is more helpful to target individuals or whole populations.

What are your views about social work services with young people who are at risk of offending? What do you think are the relative strengths and weaknesses of approaches that are explicitly aimed at work with individuals who are known offenders or who may be at risk? What do you think are the relative strengths and weaknesses of strategies that are explicitly aimed at community or *whole population* level? Start this activity by listing some of the social work practices that might fall into these two levels. Then list the potential strengths and weaknesses of each. Finally, under each heading, reflect upon and record the basis of your thoughts, for example making a note of where that knowledge or those ideas have originated from. Only by completing this last step of the activity, can you claim that your practice is based on evidence and knowledge of 'what works'.

Chapter summary

Throughout this chapter, you have been developing your understanding about development through the life stage known as adolescence. Your reading and studying have been undertaken within the context of contemporary policies and national strategic developments that aim to *make sure that all young people are given the best chance in life to succeed* (DfES, 2005, page 1).

The chapter has been structured into three main sections which reflect key themes in the national strategy. These sections have afforded you the opportunity to:

- evaluate the importance that meaningful empowerment and choice can have on young people's lives;
- consider how young people develop into adulthood as citizens; and
- explore perceived complexities and diversities in adolescence.

Additionally, the extracts, analysis and reflective activities have drawn upon notions of continuity and change in the experience of adolescence and the significance of social inclusion and social exclusion in shaping individuals' experiences of this period of their lives.

As set out in the introduction to the chapter, the majority of readers will have personal experiences of adolescence. Therefore the aim of many of the interactive activities has been to enable you to identify and reflect upon the values and perceptions that you have developed through your life course and the potential implications for your developing social work practice. You are encouraged to keep your notes and responses to the activities as evidence building to demonstrate your commitment to professional development and personal learning.

Annotated further reading and research

Burnett, R and Roberts, C *What works in probation and youth justice: Developing evidence-based practice.* Cullompton: Willan Publishing.

If you found the subject matter in the third section of this chapter to be particularly interesting or significant to your practice with young people, you will find this book very relevant. As you have seen in this chapter, many services that support young people are adapting to considerable change at this time and are increasingly under pressure to evaluate and evidence their effectiveness, much as the final extract in this chapter has done. Each of the chapters in this book discusses the findings of specific research into probation and youth justice services and the implications for developing practice.

YoungMinds. **www.youngminds.org.uk**
On their website this national charity state that they are committed to improving the mental health of all children and young people. The website provides a wealth of information, in a clear, concise and easily accessible way. There is a section labelled *Info Centre* which provides a gateway to all their resources and there is a good search facility on the site. The site offers information aimed at young people themselves, parents and professionals. Of particular interest is the *YoungMinds Magazine* and the articles therein, which provide a source of up-to-date discussion about issues affecting the lives of young people.

The National Youth Agency. **www.nya.org.uk**
According to the information provided on their website, the National Youth Agency (NYA) was founded in 1991 and is funded primarily by the Local Government Association and relevant government departments. Their aim is to support those involved in young people's personal and social development, and to promote young people's voice, influence and place in society, thus enabling all young people to fulfil their potential within a just society. The website provides a range of resources including publications, information about policy development and details about the training and qualifications needed for work with young people.

The Prince's Trust. **www.princes-trust.org.uk**
The Trust is a charitable organisation that aims to provide support, encouragement and basic financial assistance to young people aged between 14 and 30 years, in order to help them meet their goals. Their website is colourful and easily navigated. It provides a range of resources that will be of interest to both professionals and young people.

The Russell Commission website. **www.russellcommission.org**
This website aims to provide up-to-date news and information about progress on the implementation of the recommendations of the Russell Commission, referred to earlier in this chapter.

5 Development in adulthood

ACHIEVING A SOCIAL WORK DEGREE

This chapter will begin to help you to meet the following National Occupational Standards:

Key Role 1: Prepare for, and work with, individuals, families, carers, groups and communities to assess their needs and circumstances.
• Assess needs and options to make a recommended course of action.

Key Role 2: Plan, carry out, review and evaluate social work practice, with individuals, families, carers, groups, communities and other professionals.
• Work with groups to promote individual growth, development and independence.

Key Role 6: Demonstrate professional competence in social work practice.
• Research, analyse, evaluate, and use current knowledge of best social work practice.

It will also introduce you to the following academic standards as set out in the social work subject benchmark statement:

3.1.2 The service delivery context
• The significance of legislative and legal frameworks and service delivery standards.

3.1.4 Social work theory
• Research-based concepts and critical explanations from social work theory and other disciplines that contribute to the knowledge base of social work, including their distinctive epistemological status and application to practice.
• The relevance of sociological perspectives to understanding societal and structural influences on human behaviour at individual, group and community levels.

3.2.2 Problem solving skills
3.2.2.2 Gathering information
3.2.2.3 Analysis and synthesis
3.2.2.4 Intervention and evaluation

3.2.3 Communication skills
• Listen actively to others, engage appropriately with the life experiences of service users, understand accurately their viewpoint and overcome personal prejudices to respond appropriately to a range of complex personal and interpersonal situations.

3.2.4 Skills in working with others
Involve users of social work services in ways that increase their resources, capacity and power to influence factors affecting their lives.

Introduction

The focus for this chapter is human development in adulthood. The chapter includes a range of theory, academic texts, research and policy documents to enable you to reflect upon examples of the available knowledge base on the subject, particularly in relation to your own experiences and social work practice. It is likely that you, like most readers of this text, will define yourself as an adult. Therefore this chapter is about you, me and all of us. The topic should not be an abstract or complex concept.

The chapter is divided into three main sections and uses the examples of developing as an adult with a physical disability or a learning disability within our society.

Each section of the chapter raises key reflective questions which will help you to:

- consider how theories from different perspectives define adulthood and whether these approaches explain the constructions of adulthood and adult development in contemporary society;
- analyse the ways in which people may differ in their growth and development across the adult phase of the life course, using examples from research to evaluate why individuals may experience their adult lives in very different ways;
- explore a particular model of social work practice, reflecting upon how policy, research and theory can provide the knowledge base for best social work practice.

Throughout the chapter you will be encouraged to think about many different aspects of human life course development, taking account of, for example, cognitive, emotional, physical and social development in adults. Additionally, through your exploration of examples of national policies, research and academic texts, you will be prompted to consider the impact of difference. In other words, you will be prompted to evaluate the influence of gender, ethnicity, social class, race and disability on adult life course development and to reflect continually throughout the chapter, on how your learning from this impacts on your own social work practice. Before reading further, you may also find it helpful to revisit Chapter 1, which provides an overview of the life course perspective and the many potential influences upon an individual's development.

As you work through this chapter, you will be contrasting theories and evaluating the strengths and weaknesses of different explanations from research-based concepts and policy documents. You will also be looking at how this knowledge base can contribute to best social work practice with adults. Particular areas of exploration in this chapter will include the construction of adulthood, similarities and differences in adult life course development, and how theories can be used to develop social work practice.

As with other chapters, it is suggested that throughout your reading and work on this chapter, you maintain notes and records of your progress. These may take a range of different formats to suit your learning needs and your stage of professional development. Your reading and activity on this chapter will provide evidence of how you can use reflection and critical analysis to continuously develop and improve your social work practice, drawing appropriately on theories, models, knowledge and research. Further guidance and advice are given in Chapter 7 of this book.

A common theme running through this chapter is the way that each section, in some way, draws out the significance of similarities and differences in the life course development pathways of adults. Before you immerse yourself into the detailed extracts and commentary in the chapter, read through the statistical information, given below, as this provides some context about the our society, which forms the backdrop for many of the discussions.

Below are selected extracts from a government website that provides commentary information about the 2001 Census. Census day was 29 April 2001. As the National Office for Statistics states *census data gives a snapshot picture of the country at this time.*

- Just over half the adult population (aged 16 and over) is married or re-married, while over 30 per cent remain single (never-married). Separated or divorced people make up 10.6 per cent, while widowed people make up 8.4 per cent.
- Nearly 30 per cent of adults aged 16–74 in England and Wales have no qualifications. In the North East this reaches 34.7 per cent and in the West Midlands borough of Sandwell it is 45.5 per cent.
- In England and Wales, 1.1 per cent of people are Black Caribbean, 0.9 per cent are Black African and a further 0.2 per cent are from Other Black groups.
- Black Caribbeans form more than ten per cent of the population of the London boroughs of Lewisham, Lambeth, Brent and Hackney. Over ten per cent of Southwark, Newham, Lambeth and Hackney are Black African. More than two per cent of people describe themselves as Other Black in Hackney, Lambeth and Lewisham. Chinese people form more than two per cent of the population in Westminster, Cambridge, City of London and Barnet. The largest proportions of people of Mixed origin are in London, with the exception of Nottingham, where two per cent of people are Mixed White and Black Caribbean.
- More than 1.5 million households are overcrowded in England and Wales. 12 per cent of households are on the first floor or above. Nearly 41 per cent of households in the Isles of Scilly do not have central heating and 1 per cent of households in London do not have their own toilet or bath.
- Census data also show that almost 9.5 million people (18.2 per cent) say they have a long-term illness, health problem or disability which limits their daily activities or the work they could do. Of these, 4.3 million are of working age (16–64 for men; 16–59 for women), more than 1 in 8 of the age group.

(**www.statistics.gov.uk/census**)

As stated above, these are selected quotations from a government website that has taken statistical data collected from the national census and has provided a selected commentary on that data. Note the use of the word 'selected', twice in the last sentence! Whilst these figures provide significant information to reflect upon, the whole picture, the narrative accounts and background circumstances that lie behind this information is not provided. In Chapter 7 of this book, there is more discussion about the ways in which you might critically evaluate different research data. For now, reflect on this information and consider what it could tell you about adulthood and development across the life course in our society at this time. Additionally, you may be interested to explore the commentary further by visiting the website, where there is much more information and data available. As you read later sections in this chapter, for example, in respect of disabled adults, this Census information will again be relevant.

Constructing understandings of adulthood

In this section you will explore a range of different theoretical perspectives that attempt to explain the concept of adulthood and adult life course development. The reflective questions that you should consider as you read through this section are:

- what do the theoretical perspectives tell me about how adulthood is defined and given meaning in our society?
- what does this knowledge tell me about the similarities and differences in adult life course experiences?

Preparatory reading

Preparation for this section of the chapter could be undertaken by reading any text that helps you to understand theories that aim to explain life course development in adults. Here are some examples of texts that you could look at;

- Beckett, C (2002) *Human growth and development.* London: Sage. Chapter 7.
- Bee, H and Bjorklund, B (2004) *The journey of adulthood.* 5th edn. New Jersey: Pearson Education. Chapter 2.
- Crawford, K and Walker, J (2003) *Social work and human development.* Exeter: Learning Matters. Chapter 2.
- Hunt, S (2005) *The life course: A sociological introduction.* Basingstoke: Palgrave Macmillan. Chapter 1.

Extract

Bee, H and Bjorklund, B (2004) *The Journey of Adulthood*. 5th edn. New Jersey: Pearson Education, pp32–3, 'Conceptual organization of theories'.

Twenty-five years ago, any discussion of theories of adult development would have been almost totally dominated by one theory: Erik Erikson's model of psychosocial development. Erikson's view is still highly influential, but today there has been a real flowering of ideas, some of them distinctly different from Erikson's model. This wide variety of existing theories will form a better framework for later discussions if I organize the approaches along several dimensions, as I have done in Figure 2.1. Any categorization scheme, including this one, is inevitably an oversimplification. Each theory contains its own unique combination of ideas. But I can still use the two dimensions shown in Figure 2.1 as one helpful basis for organizing the options.

The first dimension on which theories may be organized is their relative emphasis on developmental progress versus developmental change. The fundamental difference, as I am using the terms *progress* and *change* in this book, is that **theories of developmental progress** assume that there is some goal or endpoint toward which the adult moves, and that this endpoint is potentially better or more mature than what is seen at earlier ages. **Theories of developmental change**, in contrast, assume no such endpoint or goal nor any improvement or growth. Among developmental theorists, for example Erikson talks about ego integrity as being the final stage, accompanied by wisdom. Vaillant describes a developmental continuum from immature to more mature forms of defense mechanisms. Other theorists, such as Levinson and Pearlin, agree that significant changes take place over the adult years, but do not see those changes as leading to more integrating or more wisdom. According to change theorists, your great aunt Elsie is different from you in specific predictable ways, but she is not necessarily better (or worse).

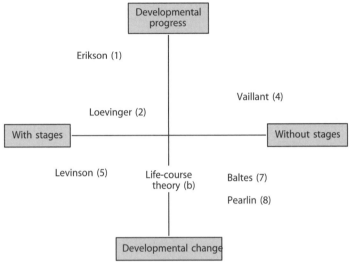

Figure 2.1

This two-dimensional grid, with development versus change as one dimension and stage versus non-stage theories as the other, allows us to contrast several of the major theories of development. (The numbers in the parenthesis indicate the sequence in which these theories are discussed in the chapter.)

The presence or absence of stages in each theory is the second dimension I have used to categorize theories of adulthood. This is a somewhat risky organizational rubric, since the term *stage* is used to describe several different concepts. Most broadly, **stage theories** refer to those that hypothesize fixed sequences of experiences or events over time, such as the family life-cycle stages I mentioned briefly in Chapter 1. More narrowly (and more commonly in psychological theories), stages imply systematic, sequential, qualitative changes in a skill or underlying psychological structure. When Piaget talks about stages in children's cognitive development, for example, he does not mean merely that children learn to add and subtract before they learn to multiply and divide, but rather, that the ability to multiply and divide requires fundamentally different understanding, logic, or mental structures. Each stage is thought of as being a structural whole, as having its own logic. Most (but not all) stage theories of adult development make similar assumptions about the nature of changes in adulthood.

Stage theorists also differ on the extent to which they argue that the various stages are age linked. Levinson's stages are strongly connected to specific ages, for example. whereas Loevinger's are not. At the other end of the continuum are those theorists who see no stages in adult development at all, in any sense of the term *stage*. Non-stage theories refer to those which argue against stages and assert that there are no shared midlife crises, no expectable integrity in old age. Instead, there are many pathways. many patterns, with adult life a process of constant change and flux. Between these two extremes lie a number of theorists who argue that there are sequences, but not stages. That is, there may be predictable orders or arrangements of experiences in adulthood, but these changes may not be integrated into inclusive, shared internal or external structures.

When we put these two dimensions together, as in Figure 2.1, some combinations are obviously more common than others. Stage theories of development (the upper left quadrant) have been particularly influential and continue to form an important backdrop for much of our current thinking, although they have waned somewhat in direct influence in recent years. Many current theories are to be found more toward the middle, such as the life-course theory. Indeed, a growing number of theorists and researchers have gone even further, shifting to the opposite corner, as in Pearlin's theory of psychological distress and Baltes's life-span theory.

Analysis

This extract has been selected for the start of this chapter as it provides a succinct and effective summary of the major psychosocial theories of adult life course development. The first stage in thinking through this extract should be to evaluate your own knowledge about these theories. You may feel, after reading this chapter, that you need to know more about each of the theoretical positions that the authors outline. If this is the case, you will find in the same text that Bee and Bjorkland go on to provide a clear discussion of each theory shown within their diagram.

Even if you do not have a detailed understanding of each of the theories mentioned, it is possible to examine the diagram and consider the assumptions and hypotheses that underpin these explanations of development in adulthood. In the upper left quadrant of the diagram, for example, Erikson's Theory of Identity Development and Loevinger's Theory of Ego Development are to be found. Both of these theories explain adulthood as having identifiable stages through which any individual progresses. One of the stages that Erikson outlines, which we might call 'middle adulthood', from the ages of approximately 25 years to 65 years, is the stage of 'maturity (generativity versus stagnation) (Erikson, 1995, page 607). Each of Erikson's eight stages are defined by his assertion that individuals need to negotiate 'a favourable ratio' between conflicting points (Erikson, 1995, page 600). In Erikson's own words:

> Generativity … is primarily the concern with establishing and guiding the next generation. In addition to procreativity, it includes productivity and creativity. Where such enrichment fails, a sense of stagnation and boredom ensues …
>
> (Erikson 1995, pages 607–8)

This text was originally written as a paper by Erik Erikson in 1968, but has since been published within various other texts. In this case, it has been taken from an edited book containing many papers written by Erikson. Clearly his theory was developed many years ago, so do you feel that it is still relevant to adult development in contemporary society? As you analyse Erikson's approach, look back to the statistical data arising from the 2001 status and consider how this theory might describe the development and experiences of people who are unemployed or who do not have children. You might feel that Erikson's theory is dated as people's lives and expectations have changed over the past thirty years. However, you should also consider the policy agendas of government in respect of employment, recreational activity and family policy. There will be many explanations for the political agenda which we do not have space to debate in this book. Nevertheless, these policies do say something about expectations and constructions of adult life in our society.

Moving to the upper right quadrant of Bee and Bjorklund's diagram, Vaillant's Theory of Adaptation to Life is shown. Bee and Bjorklund plot this theory towards the 'without stages', right-hand side of the diagram. This, however, is debatable as Vaillant's approach can be seen to suggest stages of development, albeit that these are less rigid than Erikson's, for example. On the other hand Vaillant's place on the vertical axis is probably less contentious as he hypothesises about the ability to use coping mechanisms increasing as an individual ages. Hence his theory states that adult development is progressive in nature. Vaillant suggests that, as people grow older, they become increasingly more effective and experienced in identifying the appropriate coping strategies and defence mechanisms and describes four 'adaptive mechanisms' that people use to adapt to their circumstances: mature, immature, psychotic and neurotic (Vaillant, 1977).

Vaillant's approach is often debated alongside other approaches in crisis intervention work and in Mental Health services where work is aimed at supporting individuals to develop coping strategies. Vaillant's theory is that employing *mature adaptive mechanisms* leads to a better quality of life. Do you feel that his assumptions are useful in explaining development through adulthood? In the next chapter of this book, you will explore development in later adulthood. It would be useful to carry your thinking forward to that chapter and reflect upon this model and its application to older people. How does Vaillant's approach explain crisis management in later life?

In the lower quadrants, the authors of the extract offer three theories that take a 'developmental change' stance, suggesting that we change as we grow older, but that this does not necessarily mean advancement. Paul Baltes' Life-Span Theory is a theory of human development from a psychological perspective, in which, in contrast to Erikson's approach, he does not define stages, but rather sees development as being multidimensional and multidirectional, with many and varied pathways that any individual may follow, dependent upon their life history and life context (Crawford and Walker, 2003, page 17). As you will see from your reading of Chapter 1 of this book, Baltes' concept of the life course as being multidimensional, complex and influenced by a range of historical and contextual facets can help us to understand the intricacy of adult life in our society today.

In summary, you should consider what these theories can tell us about how we define adulthood in our society. Theories offer us frameworks, structures or charts that we can use to guide us and aid our understanding of a particular phenomenon. In social work practice, theories are useful in helping us to understand the circumstances of individuals and families and their behaviours, as well as enabling us to devise models for best social work practice. The theories of human development that you have explored in this section of the chapter are useful in that they enable discussion and clarify thinking about how adulthood is experienced, the areas of adult life where there may be similarities between individuals and those areas where adult life is experienced differently. In the next two sections of this chapter, you will consider how adulthood is potentially experienced differently by physically disabled people and people with learning disabilities.

Personal reflections

As you have been exploring the similarities and differences in adult development, consider a range of people who are roughly the same chronological age as you. If possible think about the circumstances of each of the following:

* someone who is the opposite gender to you;
* someone who is a physically disabled person, or a person with a learning disability, or someone who has chronic ill-health;
* someone who is a media celebrity;
* someone from a different cultural background to you.

As far as you can tell, are you at the same physical, psychological and social point of development as each of the individuals that you have identified? If not, what are the differences and why might they be present? In what way might the theories that you have learnt about help to explain these differences? What does this tell you about understanding development in adulthood?

Comment

These are very wide-ranging and open questions and your responses will, to a large extent, depend upon your thoughts about your own physical, psychological and social development. After all, that is the starting point for your comparative reflections. There is no doubt, though, that you are likely to have listed a range of similarities between yourself and the individuals in those different circumstances, as well as potential differences. In terms of differences, you may, for example, have thought about personality differences, difference in social class or differences in opportunities available. Bee and Bjorklund (2004, page 402) remind us that *if we are to comprehend adult lives, we need to understand not only the lawfulness and order that makes us the same, but also the rules or laws that underlie the enormous diversity.*

Practical implications and activities

After reading this section of the chapter, consider the chart below. Following the two-dimensional grid developed by Bee and Bjorklund (2004, page 32) shown in the earlier extract, this activity allows *you* to theorise about life course development and plot your thoughts. If you think of the lines in Figure 5.1 as a continuum, in other words, as a range between each of the extremes, where would you put your own development as an adult, on these scales, at this time? At what point or points in your life is this position likely to vary?

Then relate this chart to the lives of adults who may use social work services. Thinking very generally, where on the line are their lives likely to be at the point of initially needing social work support? What might the aims and objectives of your intervention in their lives be? How will you use the knowledge that you are gaining to develop your practice in enabling and empowering the people you work with?

Figure 5.1 – What is adult life about?

Understanding differences in adult life course development

In the introduction to this chapter, you have seen how, from the Census statistics, there are many variations in people's circumstances and the way that they live their lives in our society today. In this section you will refer to a national policy document, research and academic literature, and look at some explanations of why this happens. The example used in this section of the chapter is that of the adult life experience of people who have physical disabilities.

The reflective questions that you should consider as you read through this section of the chapter are:

- why are there individual differences in the ways in which developing as an adult is experienced?

- why might this challenge stereotypes and assumptions, or taken-for-granted approaches?

- why is this relevant to improving and developing social work practice?

Preparatory reading

Before you read this extract, read:

- Cabinet Office (2005) *Improving the life chances of disabled people – Final report.* London: HMSO. **www.strategy.gov.uk**
  This is an executive summary document with Section1 *Independent Living* and Section 4 *Employment*, being particularly relevant to the discussion in this chapter.

- Department of Health (2005) *Independence, well-being and choice: Our vision for the future of social care for adults in England*, Cm6499. London: The Stationery Office. **www.doh.gov.uk**
  This document is a government green paper, and outlines the government's strategy for the future of social care services for adults. The full green paper is a large document over eighty pages long. However, the executive summary provides a concise synopsis of the proposals.

- Department of Health (2006) *Our health, our care, our say: A new direction for community services*, Cm6737. Norwich: The Stationery Office. **www.dh.gov/uk/ publications**
  This is the white paper that has followed and confirmed the policy direction in the green paper above. Again, an executive summary and 'easy read' version is available.

Extract

Grewal et al. (2004) *Making the transition: Addressing barriers in services for disabled people*. Leeds: Corporate Document Services. www.dwp.gov.uk

This qualitative study was commissioned in response to the Disability Rights Task Force's recommendations[1] regarding the need to tackle barriers to jointworking in the provision of services and support to disabled people. Based on in-depth interviews and focus groups with service users and local service providers in six local authority areas, and with central government policy officials, the research explored how and why disabled people can experience discontinuity in the provision of equipment and services at points of **transition** in their lives. It also explored how barriers to making a smooth transition might be addressed. The main types of transition covered in the research were: movement into, within and out of different educational settings; from child to adult services; into, within and out of employment; from one local authority to another, and between different living situations, including hospital, home, and different types of accommodation. The project was conducted by the National Centre for Social Research, with Disability Alliance.

Key findings
- Disabled people experienced a range of difficulties when making transitions in their lives, with the main negative impacts being delays to the service they needed, or not receiving the service at all.
- Service providers identified a range of barriers which may disrupt a smooth transition. These may originate at the central government level, local service delivery level, or both. Barriers can be grouped into **organisational/structural** issues (the way a particular service is structured can have implications for service delivery), **budgetary** issues (in particular, the way that budgetary boundaries and procedures operate between and within organisations in different sectors) and **procedural** issues (such as procedures being incompatible between organisations, procedures not being followed, or not existing in the first place).

[1] Disability Rights Task Force (1999) *From Exclusion to Inclusion: A Report of the Disability Right Task Force on Civil Rights for Disabled People*, (see recommendations 10.17 and 10.18 p195–196).

- From the service user perspective, the factors that were felt to contribute to a smooth transition were the approach of the service provider, resourcefulness of the service user, availability and flexibility of the service, and availability of information about appropriate services.
- The research identified a number of national and local initiatives in different sectors which are seeking to facilitate smoother transitions for disabled people. However, a number of possible areas for policy development, common across all sectors, were suggested to improve the process of transition. These include raising awareness of services amongst both service users and providers, increasing joint working between providers, investigating the possibility of a 'key worker' role for service users, widening already existing initiatives and policies, and ensuring new initiatives are evidence-based.

Summary of research

Background

The aim of the research was to explore how and why structural transitions in disabled people's lives can lead to discontinuity in the provision of equipment and services, and how this might be addressed.

Difficulties faced by disabled people making a transition

The two main negative impacts experienced by disabled people when making a transition in their life were not getting the service they needed (including a new need not being met, or losing an existing service), and delays in getting the service they needed. Examples of the former included a child moving to a new school who lost on-site provision of specialist therapy, and an adult moving home to a new local authority who had to give up equipment provided as an adaptation to their former home. Examples of delays in receipt of service included someone starting a new job, but not having the necessary IT equipment in place when required, and structural changes not being ready in time for the start of term, thus delaying the transition from nursery to infants' school for a child.

Alongside these negative impacts, disabled people could also find the transition process stressful. This could be caused by a lack of awareness about available support and services, uncertainty about their eligibility, and anxiety about the impact of making the transition on current and future service provision. From the user point of view, the following factors were identified as making a difference to how smooth a transition was:

- approach of service provider: their capacity to refer, co-ordination of the process including of assessments, and the level of transition planning;
- resourcefulness of the service user;
- availability of appropriate service, flexibility and transferability of service; and
- availability of information about appropriate services.

Barriers that impede the delivery of services during transitions

Interviews with a wide variety of service providers enabled the research to identify a range of barriers to smooth transitions across different service areas. Barriers were grouped by whether they had an **organisational/structural**, **budgetary** or **procedural** basis.

Organisational/structural: the way that some services were organised or structured could lead to discontinuity at points of transition. Key barriers identified in this area were:

- the division of a service between sectors or organisations (for example, housing adaptations provided by both housing and social services) can lead to a lack of understanding between organisations about their role and purpose, as well as a lack of information-sharing about users. In turn this can lead to delays for a user and confusion over the process of accessing a service;
- demarcation of service delivery according to team structures: the division of professional staff into different delivery teams (for example, 'child' teams, or 'mental health' teams) could have a variable impact for the service user, depending on how the team 'boundary' fitted with their particular needs. On the one hand, it could bring greater co-ordination for the service user; however, if the service user's needs cut across team boundaries, there could be a risk of poorer co-ordination of service delivery;
- flexibility of staff roles and responsibilities: there was a perception in some sectors that roles of professional staff were perhaps too fixed and that a more flexible approach towards carrying out assessments, or other aspects of service delivery would lead to fewer delays and discontinuities for the service user. Related to this, there was a debate around the extent to which the roles of professional staff should be designed to be based around specialist skills or more generalist skills. A specialist approach might give a more focused service, but perhaps involve a longer delay for the user if there were limited numbers of specialist staff. A more generalist approach might involve a quicker contact for the user, but perhaps would be more simplistic in its view.

Budgetary: Budget boundaries and regulations governing the delivery of services had implications for making transitions. The key barriers identified in this area were:

- existence and management of budget boundaries: having to fund related services from separate organisational budgets could lead to delays in provision of service or equipment;
- consequences of financial year planning: if an application for a service (for example adaptations to a home) came at a point when the annual budget was virtually accounted for, then this could cause a delay while waiting for the new financial year;
- inconsistency in scope or application of budget criteria: there could be differences in the way that criteria to determine service provision were applied i) between local authorities and ii) between different staff administering the same budget. This could lead to variability of experience for service users, but also might lead to changes in receipt of service, for example following a move across a local authority boundary;
- requirement for prioritisation due to limited budgets: a user who ends up being lower priority would be likely to have to wait longer for a service, or perhaps not get the service they would have liked;
- limited funds available for joint working: joint working arrangements were said to involve considerable time and resources, especially in getting them established;
- shortages of resource (for example qualified staff or suitable housing stock) were felt to hinder the ability to provide speedy and smooth transitions for service users.

Procedural issues creating barriers to smooth transitions included:

- difficulties for users and other providers in finding out about a service: where users or service providers were not aware of the relevant service or did not know how to go about applying for it, it created an obvious barrier to accessing the most suitable service;
- the effects of multiple assessments or duplication of assessments: where a service or similar service was delivered by two different organisations or two teams, this could result in more than one assessment, meaning a likely delay and probable confusion for the user;
- missing information or missing professional staff at assessments: not getting an appropriate service following a transition could come about because the full information was not provided at an assessment. Insufficient sharing of information came about through lack of liaison between service providers, and lack of knowledge of each other's roles;
- insufficient liaison between organisations (and between local authorities) to manage and coordinate changes in user needs: ongoing changes in user needs could result in lack of appropriate service response when there was not enough pro-active contact and liaison between service providers;
- lack of planning and preparation for predictable transitions, such as moves between schools.

What is being done to address barriers
A range of national policies and initiatives are designed specifically to help facilitate transitions and overcome some of the barriers identified in this report. Examples of these include Connexions, which aims to assist in making smooth and effective transitions from childhood through to adult activities, the Integrating Community Equipment Services initiative, which aims to bring together key agencies in the delivery of equipment by pooling of health and social services equipment stocks and budgets, and Access to Work, providing advice and practical support to enable a disabled person to make a transition into work, or to stay in work.

There were also numerous examples of work being done locally to address some of the barriers to smooth transitions. These included the design of joint procedures to reduce duplication of assessments by health and social services, and creation of multi-disciplinary teams involving social services and housing to improve coordination of services.

Issues to consider for policy development
The report identified sector-specific issues for policy development that may ease the process of transition, but also broader areas for development which are common across all policy areas and sectors. The latter include:

- **raise awareness of services** among service providers so they can make appropriate referrals, and also among service users so that they know what to apply for. Alongside this, increased user choice and control over the process is likely to result in more successful (or at least less frustrating) transitions;
- **increase 'joint working'**: although procedures and structures appear to be beginning to reflect moves towards joint working, there is scope for improvement here. Working

collaboratively, carrying out joint assessments, setting up joint procedures, or joint teams that can pool budgets – all these should help to smooth a transition process for a service user. However, joint working can entail a financial cost, and this needs to be considered when developing ideas;

- **'key worker' role**: allocating someone to manage and co-ordinate the process (a 'key worker') can ease the process for the user and appears to help create a more positive outcome;

- **widen existing initiatives and policies**: there is scope among some programmes to widen their remit in order to assist more people with transitions, for example broadening employment programmes to include help with routes to self-employment, or ensuring that disabled young people who do not have a Statement nonetheless receive the additional support they need during a transition;

- **focus on evidence-based initiatives and policies**: a concern voiced among respondents was that the need to be seen to be innovative in new initiatives could mean that insufficient attention was given to existing good practice. There is greater scope for new initiatives to demonstrate how they are building In existing effective approaches.

Analysis

The extract provides a summary of the background and the key findings of a research study that has been carried out from a qualitative approach, which means that it has been *concerned to understand individuals' perception of the world* (Bell, 1999, page 7). You should, therefore, be mindful that every element of the research will have involved interpretation, which will have been influenced by the values and experiences of those involved. That being said, however, the purpose and context of the research have been made explicit, thus enabling you to consider the possible impact of bias or value assumptions. It can be argued that qualitative data of this type is weakened as individual accounts may be tainted by subjectivity and unrelated issues. The counterargument is that this is the very strength of qualitative research, in that it provides strategies and methods that take account of the subjects' (in this case disabled people and service providers) perspectives, which are central to the questions being investigated (Morrison, 2002).

One of the pre-reading suggestions for this section is a strategic government report which sets out to *bring disabled people fully within the scope of the 'opportunity society'* (Cabinet Office, 2005). The implication of this is that, as yet, disabled people are not socially included. Indeed the research extract above would confirm this assumption. Whilst the research only relates to one aspect of disabled people's lives, namely access to services, the key findings indicate a number of complex barriers that disabled people may experience. You should note that the research was undertaken before the publication of the strategy document or the green paper or subsequent white paper. It is therefore interesting to bring the documents together and consider the ways in which research of this type may inform national strategic policy developments. For example, as you will note, the white paper *Our health, our care, our say: A new direction for community services* (DoH, 2005) incorporates a specific objective related to easier access to services. You may find it helpful to access the full research report, available via the Internet, in order to make further connections.

In the extract, it can be seen that the research has identified a number of barriers that service providers suggest may impact upon the experiences of disabled adults during periods of transition in their lives. It could be argued that these barriers explain why people with disabilities may experience aspects of their lives differently to people without disabilities. Taking the *budgetary issues* barrier as an example, the findings draw attention to the possibility that organisational budget boundaries and regulations may result in the delays, inconsistencies and resource shortages described by disabled adults. In what appears to be a potential resolution or response to this difficulty, the government strategy document *Improving the life chances of disabled people* sets out a plan to *achieve independent living by moving progressively towards individual budgets for disabled people.* This seemingly radical approach to independent living and the provision of support services is not yet fully developed and the Department of Health have instigated pilot projects that are part of the development process. The introduction of *individual budgets* and their interface with other initiatives, such as the Independent Living Funds (**www.ilf.org.uk**) and direct payments, is also set out within the white paper *Our health, our care, our say: A new direction for community services* (DoH, 2006).

As part of your learning, you should reflect upon ways in which this research and the government's policy rhetoric might challenge stereotypes, assumptions, taken-for-granted approaches, or social constructions of the experience of being a disabled adult. As you have read, the discussion above and the research extract raise the notion of *structural barriers* giving rise to a range of difficulties that disabled people face in our society. This reflects the fundamental perspective of the Social Model of Disability, which has been linked to theories of oppression (Oliver, 1990; Oliver, 1996). The Social Model of Disability perceives disability as *a consequence of the failure of social organisation to take account of the differing needs of disabled people and remove the barriers they encounter* (Oliver, 1996, page 42). Priestley (2000), who offers a critique of how social policy interprets and constructs disability within the life course, argues that the prevailing discourse of care, individualism, dependence and risk result in *the image of the non-disabled, white, heterosexual, male adult* being *central to the idealised life course constructions inherent in British Social Policy.* Therefore, it can be seen that the Social Model of Disability goes some way to answering the question raised at the start of the chapter in respect of the reasons why there are individual differences in the ways in which developing as an adult is experienced.

Personal reflections

In the preface to the green paper *Independence, well-being and choice: Our vision for the future of social care for adults in England* (DoH, 2005, page 3), Tony Blair states that *we must continue adapting this support to ensure it meets people's expectations of a high-quality service and their aspirations for independence.*

As you reflect on individual differences in adulthood and why this knowledge is important for the development of best social work practice, consider your own expectations of adult life. Make two lists:

• in the first list, record all the things that you expect from a high-quality service, not necessarily a social care service, but any service that you use;

- in the second list, note down firstly the areas of your life in which you feel you have independence, then note down those areas in which you might wish to be more independent.

Read through both your lists and, if possible, share and discuss your lists with a colleague. Reflect upon whether different people's list of expectations would show much variation. Then consider the list of areas of independence and aspirations for increased independence. Is this likely to vary between individuals? Which parts of the list might be different and why?

Comment

It is likely that making the first list was relatively straightforward for you and that, if you had the opportunity to share your list with a colleague, there will have been many similarities. For example, I would guess that, whilst you may not have used the same terminology, aspects such as good information, courtesy, respect, punctuality, flexibility, cost effectiveness and honesty may have been part of your list. Perhaps these could be summarised by the colloquial phrase 'it should do what is says on the tin'!

Completing the second list may have been more challenging, depending on how you perceive your life at this time. Perhaps if I had phrased the question differently and asked what your aspirations for the future were, you would have found this easier to respond to. It is likely though, that in some way, areas such as career aspirations or personal aspirations related to development within your close family or social networks featured in your thoughts. Whatever your responses to this part of the activity, it would be helpful if you could question yourself further and think about why you prioritise these areas of your life. Priestley (2000, page 430) suggests that for disabled people, two issues are central: work and parenting. He proposes that this is because *idealised constructions of adulthood emphasise parenting and partnering as a signifier of adult status.* Do you think that your aspirations are driven by socially constructed expectations?

Having considered your expectations from a high quality service and your own potential aspirations for further independence, the next activity follows on by asking you to think about the practical implications of your learning, in particular about the types of 'outcomes' that people may desire from social care services.

Practical implications and activities

The government white paper *Our health, our care, our say: A new direction for community services* (DoH, 2006) outlines a set of seven outcomes for people's lives that social care should support, as listed below:
- improved health and well-being;
- improved quality of life;
- making a positive contribution;
- exercise of choice and control;
- freedom from discrimination or harassment;

- economic well-being;
- personal dignity.

Additionally, research was undertaken that looked at ways of incorporating an outcome-focused approach in social work assessment and review practices with disabled adults between the ages of 18 and 65 years (SPRU, 2005). This was developed using an 'outcomes framework' which is reproduced below.

Autonomy outcomes	Personal comfort outcomes
Access to all areas of the home Access to locality and wider environment Communicative access Financial security	Personal hygiene Safety/security Desired level of cleanliness of home Emotional well-being Physical health
Economic participation outcomes	**Social participation outcomes**
Access to paid employment as desired Access to training Access to further/higher education/employment Access to appropriate training for new skills (e.g. lip reading)	Access to mainstream leisure activities Access to support in parenting role Access to support for personal secure relationships Access to advocacy/peer support Citizenship

Adapted from SPRU (2005).

Figure 5.2 The outcomes framework

- Looking at the outcomes listed above and those incorporated into the research project, can you see similarities? Are there any significant areas missing from either one?
- How do these compare with your own list of areas of independence, completed in the earlier activity?
- In what ways could this outcomes framework be used within social work practice processes?
- How might knowledge of these outcomes inform and change your social work practice with disabled adults?

Exploring models of social work practice with adults

In this chapter you have been exploring development in adulthood, firstly by considering particular theoretical perspectives that largely suggest similarities or predictable themes in adult development. The second section then analysed policy and research that suggests there are significant differences in adult development experiences for some people in our society. In order to draw together these notions of similarity and difference, we will now look at a particular approach to social work practice with adults who have learning disabilities that, arguably, both takes account of predictable similarities in people's life courses, and recognises and values difference – a person-centred approach to planning.

This chapter started with reference to Census information that reveals a rich and diverse society. The *Valuing people – A new strategy for learning disability for the 21st century* white paper (DoH, 2001c) incorporates statistical data, specifically about people with learning disabilities in contemporary British society. This too exposes significant variations in people's circumstances. The white paper estimates that *there are about 120,000 people with severe and profound learning disabilities* and *some 1.2 million people with mild/moderate learning disabilities in England.* It goes on to state that national statistics show significant variation in both service availability and service quality across the country. Additionally, in research, referred to in the green paper, Mir et al. (2001) conducted a scoping study of services for people with learning difficulties from minority ethnic communities. In the introduction to their research report, Mir et al. highlight the following points:

- minority ethnic communities face substantial inequalities and discrimination in employment, education, health and social services;
- the higher prevalence of learning difficulties in South Asian communities has been linked to high levels of material and social deprivation. These may combine with other factors such as poor access to maternal health care, misclassification and higher rates of environmental or genetic risk factors;
- people with learning difficulties from minority ethnic communities experience simultaneous disadvantage in relation to race, impairment and, for women, gender. Negative stereotypes and attitudes held by service professionals contribute to the disadvantage they face.

(Mir et al., 2001)

As well as highlighting the issues faced by people with learning disabilities, the *Valuing people* document focuses on setting out a *new vision*, with key principles and objectives. It is within the stated principle of *choice and control* that the focus of this section of the chapter, 'A person-centred approach to planning' is introduced.

The reflective questions that you should consider when learning about theories and models of practice generally, but particularly as you read through this section of the chapter are:

- how has this approach been developed and influenced?
- how does this approach inform social work practice?
- how will you learn from this knowledge and apply it to your own practice?

Preparatory reading

Before you read this extract, read:

- Department of Health (2001c) *Valuing people – A new strategy for learning disability for the 21st century,* Cm5086. London: The Stationery Office. **www.doh.gov.uk**
  This is a government white paper and as such is a fairly large document, although

it is very readable and straightforward to follow. The key section to read to prepare yourself for the learning in this section is Chapter 4, in particular pages 49–50 where 'a person-centred approach to planning' is outlined.

Extract

Brewster, J. and Ramcharan, P. (2005) Enabling and supporting person-centred approaches in Grant et al. (eds) (2005) *Learning disability: a life cycle approach to valuing people.* **Buckingham: Open University Press. Pages 491–514. This extract pages 496–8 'Person-centred care'.**

It is important to identify the specific meaning of person-centred care as conceptualized under the present policy framework of *Valuing People* (Department of Health 2001a, 2001b). At its very heart Coyle and Williams (2000: 452) make the suggestion that person-centred care is about 'valuing people as individuals', an interesting definition given the title of the learning disability White Paper in England and Wales and the fact that Coyle and Williams' work was in a different case sector.

However, as is often the case within professional, academic and service settings, such terms are adopted and used in a variety of ways. The resultant arguments about how an ideal might be thought about or operationalized in practice therefore lead to little agreement. Such is the case with person-centredness where, in their systematic review of quantitative studies on patient-centredness, Mead and Bower (2000) point out that there is very little consensus on its meaning. Person-centred care has therefore been categorized and defined in a number of ways:

- *By its 'constituent parts'*: in this approach a number of characterizing features are variously identified. For example, involvement in decision-making (Grol *et al.* 1990; Winefield *et al.* 1996); 'responsiveness to need' (Laine and Davidoff 1996); sharing of power and responsibility (May and Mead 1999); communication and partnership, empathy, health promotion, clarity and representing personal interests (Little *et al.* 2001); use choice (Barclay 1998); and patient-as-person (Kitwood 1997).

- *In terms of perspective and discipline*: in relation to primary care there is a move towards person-centred care and away from the traditional doctor–patient relationship and doctors seeing the individual solely in terms of biological pathology (see e.g. Gerteis *et al.* 1993; Little *et al.* 2001). Others have similarly written about its applicability in secondary health care settings (e.g. Coyle and Williams 2000). Different perspectives have been brought to understanding how person-centred care might operate. Coyle and Williams (2000) see it in terms of 'a personal identity threat'; others see it in terms of a 'biosocial model', emphasizing the 'experiencing individual' as the centre of decision-making (Smith and Hoppe 1991) or in terms of a model of 'egalitarianism' between doctor, service worker and patient/client or user (May and Mead 1999).

- *In relation to its outcomes*: there are a growing number of studies in this area following on from the different approaches taken in practice settings, (see e.g. Martin and Younger 2000; Mead and Bower 2000; Parley 2001).

The mish-mash of competing perspectives therefore suggests a recurrent academic fate. The concept is dismembered and then one part is taken to define it (e.g. out of all the possible things it might be there is a focus on, say, 'responsiveness to need' or 'involvement in decision-making'), or it is applied in different settings and loses it specific meaning to the area under discussion (e.g. in relation to the doctor–patient relationship).

We would argue, however, that there are some rather specific and unique intentions in adopting the idea of person-centredness within contemporary learning disability policy. These are perhaps best understood by working through some examples of the ways in which such an approach might be operationalized within the present policy context.

Valuing People (Department of Health 2001a), which represents current policy for England and Wales, places PCP at the heart of service provision and objectives. In later guidance (Department of Health 2001b: 12), person-centred planning is defined as:

> A process of continually listening and learning, focusing on what is important to someone now and in the future, and acting upon this alliance with their family and friends. The listening is used to understand a person's capacities and choices. Person-centred planning is the basis for problem-solving and negotiation to mobilise the necessary resources to pursue a person's aspirations. These resources may be obtained from someone's own network, service providers or from non-specialist and non-service sources.

It is rare now to see, for example, an advert for a position in learning disability services which does not ask for an understanding of and a commitment to person-centred care and PCP. It is the fulcrum around which nurses and other service personnel will be organizing to support clients to achieve independence, inclusion, dignity and respect in the coming years.

PCP is seen as a 'process' rather than an event. It is not a one-off meeting with a review every six months but, rather, a way of thinking and acting together. It is based on a number of assumptions that have been set out in texts on person-centred care (see Sanderson 2000 for a review). For Sheard (2004: 2), '… person centred care is a life philosophy – an aspiration about being human, about pursuing the meaning of self, respecting difference, valuing equality, facing the anxieties, threats and guilts in our own lives, emphasising the strengths in others and celebrating uniqueness and our own 'personhood'. Sheard's definition highlights the importance of working with people in a way which recognizes and acknowledges their unique identity as people of value whatever label they have been given because of their 'difference'. It also recognizes that person-centred care and support is important for everybody – we all need support in life, we all need to feel recognized, 'celebrated', loved and respected for what we do and who we are.

Analysis

The *Valuing people* white paper, suggested as pre-reading for this section, introduces the concept of *a person-centred approach* but does not provide a great deal of detailed information about the underpinning philosophy or how it can be integrated into health and social care practices. However, the extract provided begins to put this model into context and further exploration in the same text (Brewster and Ramcharan, 2005) considers the implications of implementation.

Perhaps a starting point for an analysis of this extract and the pre-reading might be to consider the terminology used in the strategy documents. Within this you should also consider the links between this white paper and the white paper *Our health, our care, our say: A new direction for community services*, suggested as pre-reading for an earlier section of this chapter, which sets out the government's strategy for the future of social care services for adults (DoH, 2006). The common themes between the preceding green paper, whose focus is evidence in its title, *Independence, well-being and choice* and the *Valuing people* document which stresses four key principles: *rights, independence, choice and inclusion*, quickly become apparent. Additionally, within the green paper, the role of a *person-centred planning facilitator*, who supports individuals *to develop their aspirations* is outlined (DoH, 2005, page 36) *as the basis for future service plans.*

In the extract, Grant et al. open the debate about perceived policy intentions and competing perspectives inherent in the different elements and definitions attributed to the term *person-centred approaches.* A person-centred approach to planning, often shortened to PCP, is described, in the *Valuing people* white paper, as a way in which the needs, aspirations and preferences of a person with a learning disability can be taken into account (DoH, 2001c, page 49). The *process of continually listening and learning, focusing on what is important to someone now and in the future* (DoH, 2001c cited in Brewster and Ramcharan, 2005, page 497) can be seen to emanate from a humanist approach which values the interpretations that individuals make of their own lives (Payne, 2005, page 184). Humanist models, particularly those which have strong connections to the work of Carl Rogers, have had significant influence on social work practice, focusing on *the importance of the 'self' seeking personal growth* (Payne, 2005, page 186). You may also have associated PCP with the narrative or biographical approach to social work practice. In the following quotation from Sugarman (2001), the connection between the narrative approach, life course development and PCP is apparent:

> The concept of life-span development as a process of narrative construction acknowledges a person's individuality: "Each of us lives a story that is ours alone" (Salmon, 1985, p.138). It allows us each an active role in authoring our own story.
>
> (Sugarman, 2001, page 77)

The approach is not without criticism, however. For example, questions have been raised about ownership of PCP and whether individual plans can also be mechanisms for collation of information to prioritise service developments (Brewster and Ramcharan, 2005, page 509). Furthermore, the process of developing and maintaining PCPs effectively may require considerable resources. As discussed by Mansell and

Beadle-Brown (2004, cited in Brewster and Ramcharan, 2005, page 509), meetings and reviews are time consuming and potentially bureaucratic. Brewster and Ramcharan (2005), again citing the work of Mansell and Beadle-Brown, also raise the issue of staff skills and the possibility of extensive training being necessary in the implementation of PCP. You may be interested to read the more detailed critique of PCP offered by Brewster and Ramcharan (2005) which is on pages 507–12 of their text.

Finally, as you reflect on how this approach may inform social work practice, I would draw your attention to the definition of PCP extracted from Department of Health guidance, quoted in the extract above, in particular that *person-centred planning is the basis for problem-solving and negotiation to mobilise the necessary resources to pursue a person's aspirations* and that those resources may be acquired in different ways. This reflects the National Occupational Standards for social work, in particular, Key Role 2 *Plan, carry out, review and evaluate social work practice, with individuals, families, groups, communities and other professionals* and Unit 7 *Support the development of networks to meet assessed needs and planned outcomes.*

Personal reflections

You have had an opportunity to read about both the strengths and potential limitations of person-centred planning (PCP). What is your view about this?

Think about your own daily life and the routines and habits that you follow. What would be important things about your current life and your aspirations that you would want recorded if a person-centred plan was developed with you? Examples might be particular routines or times of the day when you like or dislike to do things, particular foods, clothes or toiletries that you use or dislike. Reflect whether it was easy or difficult to complete this task and how a service-user might feel when developing their person-centred plan.

Comment

Your views on PCP may reflect your own life experiences or practice experiences of using a person-centred approach or something similar. Brewster and Ramcharan (2005) suggest that it is not straightforward to implement PCP within traditionally structured services but that we should *reflect on these approaches in a positive but well-informed way while continuing to work towards a more positive future for people with learning disabilities* (Brewster and Ramcharan, 2005, page 511). You may have found it quite difficult to be really clear about your own daily rituals, as these may change according to different life events, for example, whether it is a working day or the weekend. You may have found some of these things are very personal and not always things that you would want to talk about with other people. This serves to highlight the importance of social workers having high level communication skills in order to effectively empower service-users to take control of the process.

Practical implications and activities

Reflect upon your reading of this section and any experience you may have of direct work with service users. In this activity you are being asked to consider how you might put this approach into practice with adults in order to make a difference to their experience of developing through adulthood.

- Make a list of the practical social work tasks that you think are involved in implementing a person-centred approach with a service-user. Ensure that you consider the people who need to be involved in the work and the objectives of the tasks that would be undertaken. What might your person-centred plan look like?

- How do you feel that PCP will *achieve greater choice, independence and inclusion* for people with learning disabilities as they develop through adulthood?

Chapter summary

This chapter has been about developing as an adult in contemporary society. Throughout the chapter, you will have noted the recurrent theme of similarities and differences in the life course development experiences of adults. Using examples from national policy documents, research and literature, the chapter has explored theories that explain development in adulthood and the significance of similarities and differences in the experience of adulthood and has considered a particular approach to social work that values individual experiences.

Throughout the chapter you have been prompted to reflect upon your own experiences and different explanations, drawing out the potential implications for social work practice. By making notes on your reading and by recording your responses to the practical activities you will be building evidence of your evaluations and deliberations, which will demonstrate your developing understanding of how this knowledge base can contribute to best social work practice with adults. Further guidance and advice in respect of recording, sharing and progressing your learning are given in Chapter 7 of this book.

Annotated further reading and research

Grant, G, Goward, P, Richardson, M and Ramcharan, P (eds) (2005) *Learning disability: A life cycle approach to valuing people.* Buckingham: Open University Press.
This text has been referred to extensively in the latter part of this chapter, with the final extract being taken from Chapter 6. This is a large book, 757 pages, with chapters written by different contributors. The chapters are organised into five sections, the first of which explores *The constructions of learning disability,* whilst the other chapters take the reader through the life course from childhood to ageing and end of life issues. There are particularly useful chapters on using the narrative approach with people who have learning disabilities and Part 4, which focuses on *Social inclusion and adulthood,* develops thinking around different key aspects of adult life, such as employment, community and social networks.

Sugarman, L (2001) *Life-span development: Frameworks, accounts and strategies.* 2nd edn. Hove: Psychology Press Ltd.

This second edition of Léonie Sugarman's seminal text is relevant and useful in all your human life course development studies. While not a social work book, Sugarman's final chapter discusses intervention in people's lives, focusing on the range of sources of help that may be available to people. Sugarman also presents a theoretical discussion that develops the concepts of the narrative approach as a mechanism for understanding continuity across the life course.

Mencap. **www.mencap.org.uk**
Mencap is a United Kingdom-wide charity working with people with learning disabilities and their families and carers. The organisation campaigns for equal rights and greater opportunities for people with learning disabilities and challenges attitudes and prejudice. Mencap also provides advice and support to meet people's needs throughout their lives. All areas of the website may be of interest to you, but of particular relevance to your reading in this chapter are the documents, guidance notes and briefing that Mencap provides about the implementation of person-centred planning.

6 Development in later adulthood

ACHIEVING A SOCIAL WORK DEGREE

This chapter will begin to help you to meet the following National Occupational Standards:

Key Role 1: Prepare for, and work with, individuals, families, carers, groups and communities to assess their needs and circumstances.
- Assess needs and options to make a recommended course of action.

Key Role 2: Plan, carry out, review and evaluate social work practice, with individuals, families, carers, groups, communities and other professionals.
- Work with groups to promote individual growth, development and independence.

Key Role 6: Demonstrate professional competence in social work practice.
- Research, analyse, evaluate, and use current knowledge of best social work practice.

It will also introduce you to the following academic standards as set out in the social work subject benchmark statement:

3.1.1 Social work services and service users
- The social processes (associated with, for example, poverty, unemployment, poor health, disablement, lack of education and other sources of disadvantage) that lead to marginalisation, isolation and exclusion and their impact on the demand for social work services.
- Explanations of the links between definitional processes contributing to social differences (for example, social class, gender and ethnic differences) to the problems of inequality and differential need faced by service users.
- The nature and validity of different definitions of, and explanations for, the characteristics and circumstances of service users and the services required by them.

3.1.2 The service delivery context
- The complex relationships between public, social and political philosophies, policies and priorities and the organisation and practice of social work, including the contested nature of these.
- The significance of legislative and legal frameworks and service delivery standards.

3.1.4 Social work theory
- Research-based concepts and critical explanations from social work theory and other disciplines that contribute to the knowledge base of social work, including their distinctive epistemological status and application to practice.

3.2.2 Problem-solving skills
3.2.2.3 Analysis and synthesis

3.2.4 Skills in working with others
- Involve users of social work services in ways that increase their resources, capacity and power to influence factors affecting their lives.

Introduction

In this chapter you will have the opportunity to read and reflect upon topical theory, research, policy and your own experiences in relation to human development in later adulthood and social work practice. The chapter is divided into three main sections with each section of the chapter raising key reflective questions which will help you to:

- consider research, academic texts and national policy statements that inform our understanding of the definition of later adulthood and reflect upon how our common understandings of growing older in our society are constructed. You will also examine what this can tell us about ourselves and about values and attitudes;
- explore the ways in which knowledge and understanding about transitions in later adulthood are relevant to social work practice and why individuals adapt, change and develop through life events in different ways;
- analyse how relevant theories and models explain human development in later adulthood and how these approaches can underpin and inform social work practice.

Human life course development in later adulthood has been the subject of research and exploration over many years and across many disciplines. Crawford and Walker (2003) give an overview of the theories and explanations of development and the impact of life events in this period of life, whilst also considering the implications of these explanations for social work practice. This chapter will explore particular examples of national strategy in respect of health and social care, current knowledge, research, analysis and evaluation, and enable you to consider their impact upon social work practice from a life course perspective.

The final chapter of this book discusses ways in which you might keep a record of your learning and progression through each of the chapters, particularly developing your skills in critical analysis, synthesis and reflection, but also ensuring that you can evidence the impact this learning has had on your professional development and practice with older people. You are therefore encouraged to read Chapter 7 of this book and consider the learning, sharing and recording strategies that will be most effective to meet your learning and developmental needs, before you progress further with this chapter.

Before you start reading through the different elements of this chapter, consider the following statistics which have been selected from the many facts and figures available about the lives of older people in our society. Reflect on what these figures might tell us about the position of people in later adulthood in England and the significance of the professional support and care that they receive. Additional supporting facts and figures are available from either Age Concern England **www.ageconcern.co.uk** or the Department of Health **www.doh.gov.uk**.

Statistics provided by Age Concern England, collated from National Population Projections, tell us that the number of people over pensionable age, taking account of the change in women's retirement age, is projected to increase from nearly 11.4 million in 2006 to 12.2 million in 2011. It will rise to nearly 13.9 million by 2026, reaching over 15.2 million in 2031. (**www.ageconcern.co.uk**)

In a recent policy paper, Age Concern cites data from *Social trends* to provide evidence that most older people in the United Kingdom are white. Only 4% of people over state pension age are from non-white minority ethnic groups, although proportions vary between different groups:

– 16% of white people are aged 65 or older;
– 9% of Black Caribbean people are 65 or over;
– 2% of those whose ethnic background is of Black African or mixed race are aged 65 or older.

(Age Concern, 2005, page 3)

In respect of social care services in England, community care statistics from the Department of Health state that from 1 April 2002 to 31 March 2003, 479,000 clients over the age of 65 received home help or home care services, 157,000 received day care and 189,000 received meals. In addition, the 2001 national census shows that, in England and Wales, 342,032 people aged 65 and over were at that time providing 50 hours or more of unpaid care per week. Thus, as well as being recipients of social care provision, older people are themselves providers of social care in our society. (**www. ageconcern.co.uk**)

Constructing understandings of later adulthood

In this section, through consideration of key documents, you will analyse and reflect upon what knowledge and evidence can convey about how later adulthood is constructed and given meaning in our society. This will also enable you to think about what these messages suggest about us as individuals in society and our own values and attitudes towards later life. The reflective questions that you should consider as you read through this section of the chapter are:

- what does research, academic texts and national policy tell me about how later adulthood and growing older in our society is defined and understood?
- what does this knowledge suggest about my own values and attitudes in respect of older people and growing older?

Preparatory reading

Before you read this extract, read:

- Crawford, K and Walker, J (2004) *Social work with older people*. Exeter: Learning Matters. Pages 10–11.
- Department of Health (DoH) (2001b). *The National Service Framework for older people*. London: The Stationery Office. Standard 1, pages 16–21.

Extract

Godfrey, M, Townsend, J, and Denby, T (2004) *Building a good life for older people in local communities: The experience of ageing in time and place*, **Ref 041. York: Joseph Rowntree Foundation www.jrf.org.uk**

This study is about the experience of ageing. Older people talked about their lives, described the opportunities and challenges of getting old, and shed light on what makes for a 'good life'. A significant aspect of the study, by Mary Godfrey, Jean Townsend and Tracy Denby at Leeds University, was partnership with older people's groups in Leeds and Hartlepool which participated in interviewing, analysing and shaping the report. The study found that:

- Ageing is not just about decline, nor even about maintaining an even keel. It is also about seeing and seizing opportunities and actively managing transition and loss. However, there is considerable variation in the resources available to people to deal with changes that accompany ageing.
- Central to a 'good life' in old age is the value attached to inter-dependence: being part of a community where people care about and look out for each other; a determination 'not to be a burden' especially on close family; and an emphasis on mutual help and reciprocal relationships.
- The essence of 'ageing well' is the ability to sustain inter-dependent lives and relationships that meet needs for intimacy, comfort, support, companionship and fun. Threats to life quality include not only bereavement and ill health, but 'daily hassles' and their cumulative impact.
- The localities where older people live are of enormous importance. As they get frailer, their lives are increasingly affected by, and bounded within, their immediate physical and social environments.
- Appropriate and sensitive services should reflect older people's values and capacities and their desire for an 'ordinary life': 'sufficient' and secure income, social and intimate relationships, stimulating and interesting activities, accessible and timely information, support to manage things that pose difficulties, a comfortable, clean, safe environment, and a sense of belonging to and participating in communities and wider society.
- Locality-based service models offer the potential to connect the values and preferences of older people within a network of community groups to support a 'good old age' and provide a significant bridge between communities and statutory services. The experiences and views of older people offer insights into the services and support needed to sustain their well-being.

Introduction

This study was carried out in partnership with two groups of older people. Located within an ethnically diverse, inner city area of Leeds, Caring Together is one of thirty-seven neighbourhood networks in the city that support and engage older people. The Retired Resource Network in Hartlepool brings together retired people to provide mutual support and to campaign around issues of relevance to them.

The study, undertaken between 2001 and 2003, employed in-depth interviews, focus groups and participant observation. One-to-one interviews, based on a life history approach, were held with eighty-four people ranging in age from 58 to 97 of different experiences and abilities. Eleven focus group interviews, involving people known to each other (ninety-eight individuals) were held to deepen understanding of life in older age and strategies for managing change. Six focus groups (fifty-eight people) later explored service preferences and priorities. At one site, four older people and community staff members undertook half the individual interviews and were actively involved in all stages of the study, including analysis and shaping the report.

The questions guiding the study were:

- What makes for a 'good' life in old age?
- How is this affected by the localities where people live and their social characteristics and circumstances (gender, ethnicity and physical ability)?
- What kinds of services and support can sustain well-being as people age?

Understanding older people

Even the frailest people invested time and energy in taking responsibility to look after themselves. They experienced frustration when professionals and agencies appeared neither to understand their contribution nor even value their expertise about their needs.

In managing day-to-day, older people sought to prioritise those things that were important to them and identified a need for help either to compensate for what they could not do or to enable them to continue with what was valued. However, there was often a mismatch between what services provided and what people viewed as a need. Often it was a case of selecting the least negative option, because of the way services were rationed or delivered.

A partnership between older people, professionals and service providers has to start from an understanding of what is important to older people and build upon their abilities and resources in managing difficulties. An understanding of the person in terms of their whole life is also significant.

Conclusions

Securing well-being in old age requires understanding and action at different levels: individual, neighbourhood/community and society. At each level, the capacities of older people represent an undervalued resource, not only in securing a better life for themselves, but in contributing to the building of sustainable neighbourhoods for everyone. The research highlighted that it is counterproductive to view ageing as a constellation of 'problems' that require 'interventions'. Rather, the findings highlighted older people's resilience in the face of difficulties and their capacity, with proper resources, for organising themselves and devising their own solutions.

Analysis

There is no one accepted definition of later adulthood, thus the boundaries of this concept can be debated. For example, the National Service Framework for older people suggests that *people as young as 50* are *entering old age* (DoH, 2001b, page 3), whilst 99% of the participants of the research project detailed in the extract were aged 60 years or over. A recent Audit Commission report (2004a) commences by clarifying the complexity of attempting to categorise *older people*. The report states that:

> Older people are an enormously diverse group, ranging from people who are in mid-life to those who have reached their centenary and beyond ... chronological age is increasingly inadequate as a measure of health or activity. ... The diversity of older people extends well beyond age, to encompass ethnicity, income, sexuality, interests and life experience. Any response to older people therefore needs to be tailored to the needs and aspirations of individuals.
>
> (Audit Commission, 2004a, page 3)

In the Joseph Rowntree Foundation (JRF) research, Godfrey et al. adopt a life course approach to their study and conclude that *there are facets of ageing that are common to us all* but that, through the stories and experiences of older people themselves, it is clear that *the experience of ageing is also significantly shaped and influenced by the wider social context of people's lives.* (2004, page 211). Thus whilst the notion of diversity is very evident in the extract from the JRF research, the findings of this study reveal much more about older people and their values and attitudes. The value of *interdependence* is one example that is evident from this research. *Interdependence* refers to a wide range of social relationships, networks and support. Gergen and Gergen (in Gubrium and Holstein, 2003, pages 206–7) suggest that *interpersonal relationships* and *contributions to community* are two of the key themes that contribute to a positive later life. Thus involvement with family, friends and a network of social relationships can be significant for older people.

In terms of social work practice, the National Occupational Standards for social work, Key Role 2, states that social workers must *support the development of networks to meet assessed needs and planned outcomes* and *interact with individuals, families, carers, groups and communities to achieve change and development to improve life opportunities*. These different levels of action, illustrated below, are also reflected in Godfrey et al.'s conclusions, as you will see at the end of the extract you have read.

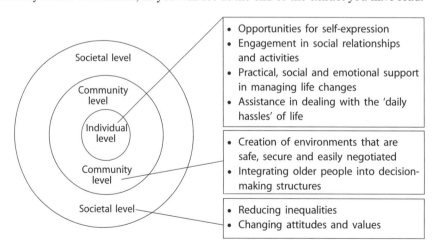

Developed from Godfrey et al. (2004, page 228)

Figure 6.1 Levels of action to secure well-being in later adulthood

Another theme evident in these research findings is the value of *independence* supported by *appropriate and sensitive services*. The report acknowledges that professional or formal support services are only one element of the resources that older people use, but that accessing such services can cause difficulties, with issues raised such as ageism, lack of respect and being ignored and stereotyped. Indeed, the document suggested here as pre-reading, the *National Service Framework for older people* (DoH, 2001b) Standard 1, would suggest that there is much to be done to eradicate age discrimination within services for older people. The more recent white paper *Our health, our care, our say: A new direction for community services* (DoH, 2006) encompasses a specific goal of tackling inequalities and improving access to services. As you work through this chapter, it is recommended that you undertake a further search of the government's national publications that have followed and provided more detailed guidance on this National Service Framework (NSF) for example, the recent *Review of progress against National Service Framework for older people* (Healthcare Commission, 2006) where examples of good practice in local communities are cited.

This extract has been put together from the *Research findings* document which is a summary of the full research report. The *Findings* are available on the Joseph Rowntree Foundation website and it is recommended that you read that summary of this research. Furthermore, whilst the full report is 239 pages long, it provides a fascinating insight into the experience of ageing. As this book has shown throughout, knowledge and understanding of these experiences and of people's life courses enables professionals to develop their practice, and the support and services which aim to meet people's needs and improve their quality of life.

Personal reflections

As you have seen, the research example used in this section of the chapter focuses on the experiences and perspectives of older people gathered through taking a life story approach. Hence, throughout both the summary *Findings* document and the full report on the research, there are direct quotations from some of the older people who participated in the project.

- Read the following three quotations taken from the research, where older people express their views on later life.

'*They can't know until they have been there what it is like to be old. They say, "Well you have had your innings". It's the other way round ... We have got over the rough, unpleasant stuff ... and now it is our chance ... You can't, until you are old yourself, see how precious every day is. Now is the time to enjoy yourself.*' (Miss Emsley)

'*You don't think to yourself, "I'm getting older" and in a way, you want to be the way you were. But I also want people to know that there is change taking place – but that I can still be part of things. There needs to be some acknowledgement that we are getting old but that, at the same time, we are not past it.*' (Mrs Bates)

'*Things keep throwing me back: then I start climbing again.*' (Mrs Coulter)

- Make a list of the key words that strike you as significant in these quotations. Then add additional words, if necessary, that demonstrate the types of values and attitudes that you can see being expressed by these individuals.

- Reflect upon the similarities and differences between the values, attitudes and concerns expressed by these older people and your own values, attitudes and concerns. Write a few sentences on how they compare and what the cause of the similarities and differences might be.

Comment

You may have identified a range of attitudes, opinions and thoughts emerging from these three small excerpts. For example, some of the themes that are apparent are optimism, ability, strength of character, determination and opportunity. You may also have sensed some elements of anger or defiance being expressed which could be seen to arise from concerns about the opinions and prejudices of others. These three quotations are all from women, so you should question whether a man would have other concerns. You might also question whether these comments represent difference across cultural experience. Within the full research report you will find direct quotes from a much wider range of older people. With respect to the third part of your reflections, you may have thought that many of the attributes seen within these excerpts could equally be expressed by people in earlier stages of life. You may have been surprised at the optimism and determination shown by these three individuals. Your reflections about later adulthood and these research findings will help you to appreciate how the lives and experiences of people, regardless of their age or point in the life course, will be characterised by diversity, opportunity, continuity and change.

Practical implications and activities

The final sentence in Godfrey et al.'s research concludes that:

> Focusing on ageing as representing a constellation of 'problems' that require 'interventions' ignores older people's resilience in the face of difficulties and their own capacity, with proper resources, for organising themselves and devising their own solutions – at the individual and collective level.
>
> (Godfrey et al., 2004, page 229)

Given this statement, the overall findings from this research and the National Service Framework for older people, in what ways do you think you can develop your own social work practice with older people? Also, how do you think professional social work with older people, at a broader level, can be developed and enhanced?

Understanding the impact of transitions in later life

In this section you will consider why an understanding of transitions in later life is important to social work practice, in particular reflecting upon the influences on older people's lives and how they may adjust, change and develop through life events in different ways. This will be achieved through reflection on the concepts of disengagement theory and activity theory, using retirement as an example of a transition experienced by many older people in our society. The reflective questions that you should consider as you read through this section of the chapter are:

- why is research and evidence about the impact of transitions in later adulthood important to social work practice?
- why do individual older people respond to life events or transitions in very different ways?

Preparatory reading

Before you read this extract, read:

- Sugarman, L (2001) *Life-span development: Frameworks, accounts and strategies.* Hove: Psychology Press Ltd. Chapter 6, pages 135–7.
  These pages outline types of life events and transitions. Alternatively you could revise the following:

- Crawford, K, and Walker, J (2003) *Social work and human development.* Exeter: Learning Matters. Chapter 6, pages 100–2.
  These pages also describe life events as transitions and the resources that individuals may draw on as they move through such transitions.

Extract

Hunt S (2005) *The life course: A sociological introduction.* Basingstoke: Palgrave Macmillan. Pages 188–190.

Retirement
Disengagement or Discontinuity?
Andrew Blakie maintains that in the case of the UK, the social construction of ageing has passed through three stages in the twentieth century and that these developments are largely connected with retirement and social disengagement. To begin with, the first half of the twentieth century witnessed the emergence of retirement as a mass experience. Second, this form of social disengagement culminated in its mid-century institutionalization through state legislation. Since the late 1960s, an increasing fragmentation has been evident, both as regards the time in which people leave work and in ways they spend their time afterwards in a phase of the life course which is increasing as life expectancy is extended (Blakie 1999, 59–60).

The simple explanation for the creation of retirement as an institution is that advanced technology reduces the need for everyone to work literally for life, while placing a premium on current skills implies that the older worker has to give way to the younger. By contrast to these developments in the West, in Third World societies that depend on the labour of everyone, male and female alike, and where no pension schemes exist, most people work until they are physically incapable of doing so.

In terms of a sociological framework applied to the social and economic necessity of retirement, the earliest formulated was that commonly understood as 'disengagement theory'. Cumming and Henry's variation of the theoretical paradigm is perhaps the best known, although it presents a rather negative picture of the social position of the elderly. The theory contends that social disengagement for the aged is socially and psychologically functional and a natural part of the ageing process. Thus, ageing has certain fixed repercussions which, in turn, accounts for the reasons why the elderly become marginalized from society (Cumming and Henry 1961). It is a theory which implies that the major social passage in later life is associated with 'loss' whether one of social role, status, or income.

It is clear that the disengagement theory assumes that biological ageing is a straightforward process and a detachment of older people from the workforce is constructive since deteriorating physical or mental powers undermine their economic contribution. Hence, their 'disengagement' would give way to younger people in the occupational sphere. Disengagement is thus a means by which society promotes its own orderly functioning by removing ageing people from 'normal' and productive roles while they are still performing them. There is also the additional advantage that in a rapidly changing society, young workers typically have the most up-to-date skills and training. Disengagement may advantage the elderly as well as society. Hence, it is assumed that for the most part, older people with diminished capabilities invariably welcome the opportunity for more leisure time and the freedom from the pressures of work. There is a psychological dimension too. As people age, according to the disengagement theory, their most basic social psychological need changes from one of active involvement to one of inactive contemplation about the meaning of life in the face of impending death.

Despite modifications, a number of critiques have damagingly undermined the disengagement theory – many of which are connected with broader culture conceptions related to ageing. First, it largely fails to recognize that many elderly people may not wish to disengage from productive roles since it includes loss of social prestige and brings social isolation. Second, in practical terms many of those retiring, mostly lower paid workers, cannot always readily disengage from paid work because they do not have sufficient financial security to do so. Third, there is no compelling evidence that the benefits of disengagement outweigh their cost to society, since it results in the loss of at least some human resources. Indeed, a comprehensive system of engagement would have to take into account the widely different abilities of the elderly. Fourth, retirement means the care of people who might better be able to provide for themselves. This is particularly so in an ageing society where governments are increasingly concerned about how such a large portion of the population can be supported. Finally, it is possible to argue that the elderly's contribution to society is hugely underestimated, especially because they take part in such unpaid work as childcare and participate in charity work in a voluntary capacity.

Another difficulty with the disengagement theory is that retirement is not a simple stage of adaptation but part of a process which has both positive and negative consequences. Atchley identifies various possible phases of retirement. To begin with, there is pre-retirement where, as retirement approaches, the individual begins to prepare for the experience and relevant activities. When retirement occurs the person takes one of three paths: the 'honeymoon' phase that is marked by euphoria since the individual does many of the things s/he 'never had time for before'. This phase requires money and good health. Others will move instantly to 'an immediate retirement routine' that in all probability stabilizes over time and involves scheduled activities at a regulated pace which will likely turn into a more or less permanent lifestyle. Still others will see retirement as a 'rest and relaxation' phase consisting of a very low level of activity. Many may initially adopt this but become restless and subsequently more active (Atchley 1988).

After experiencing one of these three phases during the initial retirement, movement to other phases is probable. Some people edge into a 'disenchantment phase' as they discover retirement does not live up to expectations, but this may be relatively rare. Another possibility is a 're-orientation' phase in which retired persons change their approach to retirement. Perhaps they become increasingly involved with friends and family, after initially pursuing their interests more or less on their own. But eventually the great majority of retired persons enter into the phase of 'routine'; in which they know what it is they want and are able to do – a set of stable activities often constituting a particularly lifestyle. Finally, they may adopt a – 'termination phase' and go back to the job they left or start a new one because they enjoy working or need to support themselves in old age. Eventually, however, all older people adopt the phase of routine as they settle down to live out their last years.

Analysis

Transitions are defined as phases or stages within the life course when people move through life events (Crawford and Walker, 2003). Clearly retirement and the change of social status that this brings, is a major life transition.

In this extract, Hunt (2005) provides a critique of 'disengagement theory' by applying the notion to the contemporary social and economic outcomes of retirement. Whilst this extract is not supported by research evidence, Hunt makes an effective challenge to some of the assumptions inherent in disengagement theory by applying the approach to current understandings of growing older in our society. Hunt also suggests that the meanings that we attach, or the understandings that we have of growing older (the social constructions of ageing) are influenced by the social institution of retirement. He argues that retirement is not one clear stage or transition, but is a process within which there are a number of phases. To help you understand the way in which Hunt, citing Atchley 1988, conceptualises these phases, they are represented diagrammatically in Fig. 6.2.

The notion that life course transitions can be broken down into multiple stages or smaller transitions in this way can be helpful when developing our understanding of the experiences of individuals. Similarly, Fairhurst (2003, page 31) describes the consequence of potential *movement from full-time to part-time paid work and/or to unpaid work* as being *multiple retirements*. However, Hunt also describes retirement as a predictable and intended life event, with a *pre-retirement* preparation phase. This approach fails to take account of the many varied and complex patterns of people's lives, for example, sudden, unexpected retirement or reduction in employment that may come about due to the individual's ill-health, the ill-health of a family member or redundancy. Thus there are increasingly many different pathways that people take through their lives, between paid employment and leisure activities. People now move in and out of work, changing the emphasis that they put on work, leisure and community involvement at different stages in their life course, so it could be argued that retirement is no longer the predictable life course transition that it once was (Phillipson, 1998).

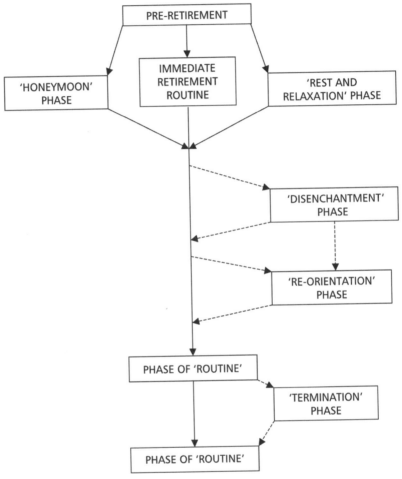

Adapted from Hunt (2005:190)

Figure 6.2 Phases of retirement (2005)

In terms of social work practice, *understanding the impact of transitions within a person's life course is important for social work practice in order to help us understand other people's lives* (Crawford and Walker, 2003, page 5). Thus the extract from Hunt provides us with a framework through which we might develop an understanding of the transition of retirement in later adulthood. However, as we have seen from the framework itself, from the analysis above and the pre-reading that you have undertaken, individuals will experience and respond to the same transition or life event in many different ways and their behaviours and the decisions they take will vary.

Therefore, whilst your practice as a social worker should be informed by knowledge of models and frameworks, such as that presented here, you should overlay this with the individual's perspective and interpretation of their own situation. In other words, through assessment and exploration, you will discover how individuals themselves theorise their passage through retirement or other transitions in their life course.

Personal reflections

In the extract, Hunt states that retirement is *part of a process which has both positive and negative consequences.* (Hunt, 2005, page 190).

What are your own thoughts about the transition of retirement from paid employment?

Using separate columns make two lists. Firstly list all of the possible negative consequences of retirement that you can think of and then make a second list, containing all of the possible positive consequences.

Take a little time to look at your first list and consider what the impact or effect of these experiences might be for an older person. How might the impact of these potentially negative outcomes be reduced?

Having thought about the possible outcomes of retirement, are there issues that Hunt has not considered, or elements of his argument that you would wish to challenge?

Comment

The research and texts that you have read so far in this chapter have shown how later life can be explained as being *simultaneously about opportunity and loss, change and adjustment* (Godfrey et al., 2004, page 211). The transition of retirement is an example that encompasses all of these concepts. In terms of the challenges or potential negative consequences of this life event, you may have considered issues of mental or emotional health such as possible reactive depression linked to loneliness, boredom and coming to terms with the later stages of life. However, as you considered the possible positive elements in this experience, you may have seen other possibilities, such as opportunities to relax and the reduction of stress caused by work pressures. Another aspect you may have drawn out is the potential impact of change in income and status. Some of the more challenging aspects of this transition could be balanced by the opportunities to develop in different ways, to take up new interests and activities, or to use experience and knowledge to assist others and participate in the community. Your reflections on this section of the chapter and the questions posed here may depend upon your own age and life course. For example, a younger person who is at the stage of planning and developing their career, may find it more difficult to see opportunities in retirement, whereas an older person, who has worked for many years, may have exciting plans for their retirement. Thus, as readers of this chapter will all have different perspectives on transitions in later adulthood, so too will older people themselves as they make those transitions.

The extract by Hunt is useful in providing a framework and a theoretical discussion about the transition of retirement, but as we have already seen, it could be criticised for not giving enough consideration to unexpected or unplanned retirement, such as that which might come about due to sudden ill health or redundancy. Another aspect that perhaps warrants further consideration is the impact of cultural diversity. Hunt touches briefly on this aspect, when he considers labour-market approaches in Third World societies (2005, page 189). However, we need to consider the experiences, perspectives and life course development of people from black and minority ethnic communities who are ageing in our society. Age Concern suggests that such recognition has been slow *resulting in the exclusion of their differing needs and issues from mainstream service provision* (2005, page 4).

There has also been research into the impact of gender on how individuals adjust to the transition of retirement. Barnes and Parry (2003) undertook research for the Policy Studies Institute to examine *the contribution that gender roles and identities make to the overall configuration of resources available to particular individuals.* They concluded that gendered identities, mediated by class and ethnic differences, have implications for how individuals approach and adapt to retirement. Ethnicity and gender though, are only two of the areas of potential diversity and the experiences, expectations and perspectives of older people will reflect a range of differences such as those based on income, social class, language, health or sexuality.

Practical implications and activities

In this section of the chapter you have explored why it is important for social workers to understand the impact of transitions in later adulthood. The transition of retirement has been used as an example here, but the issues, reflections and lessons for practice that arise from that example are relevant across all areas of social work practice with older people.

Think about the many transitions or life events that people in later adulthood may experience. Some of these may not be exclusive to later life, but their impact may be different when experienced by an older person, or where they occur together and have a cumulative effect, for example, moving house, bereavement, retirement, or physical changes. Then, taking into consideration your reading of this chapter so far, write down the strategies that you, as a social work practitioner, might employ to support, enable and assist an older person to move through these transitions.

Using theory to explain development in later adulthood

Throughout this book and in the earlier sections of this chapter, you have already studied many different theories, models and concepts that provide a range of explanations and ideas about how we develop as we grow older. As a revision of your learning, it would be useful to return to some of the earlier sections of this book where particular theories are discussed, to evaluate the applicability of some of these theories to social work practice with older people. For example, the latter section of Chapter 3, where an ecological systems approach is analysed in respect of childhood development, or Chapter 5, where psychosocial theories are discussed. In this final section of this chapter, you will look more specifically at how relevant theories and models explain human development in later adulthood and how these approaches can underpin and inform best social work practice.

The reflective questions that you should consider when learning about theories generally, particularly as you read through this section of the chapter, are:

- how does this theory explain or assist to develop social work practice? Is it relevant and applicable to social work practice?
- how can this theory or model inform and be integrated, or applied to, my future social work practice?

Preparatory reading

Before you read this extract, read:

- Payne, M (2005) *Modern social work theory.* Basingstoke: Palgrave Macmillan. Chapter 1.
  Reading this chapter will remind you of the importance of theory to social work practice and will help you to conceptualise what theory is and how it is used. If you are not able to read the whole chapter, the key section to prepare you for the next part of this chapter is the section headed *Practice and other theory*, pp5–7.

Extract

Payne, M (2005) *Modern social work theory*. Basingstoke: Palgrave Macmillan Chapter 7, pp150–3.

Germain and Gitterman: the life model

Germain and Gitterman's (1980, 1996) *life model* of social work practice is the major formulation of ecological systems theory; Germain edited a collection of articles demonstrating its application across a range of social work (1979a). She argues that there are close parallels with ego psychology in the importance given to the environment, action, self-management and identity (Germain, 1978a). However, both sets of ideas are conceptually distinct and can be used without each other.

The life model is based on the metaphor of ecology, in which people are interdependent with each other and their environment: they are 'people-in-environment' (PIE). The relationship between people and their environment is reciprocal: each influences the other over time, through exchanges. The aim of social work is to increase the *fit* between people and their environment.

Figure 7.1 sets out the life model. People are seen as moving through their own unique life course. As they do so, they experience *life stressors*, transitions, events and issues that disturb their fit with the environment. This causes an unexpected disturbance in their capacity to adapt to their environment, such that they feel that cannot *cope* with it. They move through two strategies of *appraisal* of the stressor and the stress. First, they judge how serious the disturbance is, and whether it will cause harm or loss or be a challenge. Second, they will look at the measures they might take to cope and resources they have to help them. They will try to cope by changing some aspect of themselves, the environment or the exchanges between them. Signals from the environment and their own physical and emotional responses give them *feedback* about the success of their efforts at coping.

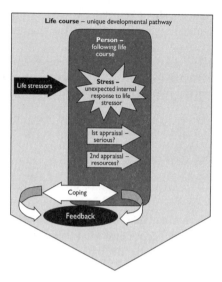

Figure 7.1 The life model of social work practice.

Among the resources that people have in order to cope are:

- *Relatedness* – the capacity to form attachments
- *Efficiency* – their confidence in their ability to cope
- *Competence* – their sense that they have relevant skills, or can get help from others
- *Self-concept* – their overall evaluation of themselves
- *Self-esteem* – the extent to which they feel significant and worthy
- *Self-direction* – their sense of having control over their lives, alongside taking responsibility for their actions while respecting others' rights.

While these are presented in relation to individuals, personal responses are markedly affected by the influence of experiences in people's families and communities. An apparently poor community, for example, may offer significant resources of self-respect. The presentation of the model may be criticised for making the fine distinctions drawn here unnecessarily detailed for everyday practice.

The ability to use these interpersonal resources is affected by social factors. These are:

- *Coercive power* – where dominant groups withhold power because of personal or cultural features of client groups
- *Exploitative power* – where dominant groups create technological pollution endangering health and well-being, especially of poor people
- *Habitat* – the physical and social settings of the client
- *Niche* – the particular social position held by the client
- *Life course* – unique, unpredictable pathways through life, and the diverse life experiences gained as a result of following them

- *Historical time* – the historical context in which the life course is experienced
- *Individual time* – the meanings that people give to their life experiences
- *Social time* – events affecting the families, groups and communities that the client is part of.

Germain's early work focused on space and time as aspects of social work practice, and these influences emerge in this element of the model. A criticism might be that, as with systems theory more broadly, these ecological metaphors do not add to the value or concepts such as social class, social status and discrimination on grounds of race and culture (Chapters 11–13), and that time is an unnecessary aspect of the three factors describing the impact of social contexts on people's relationships and personal responses to life. Ideas of social construction may deal with these concepts more effectively (Chapter 8).

The aim of practice in the life model is to improve the fit between people and their environment, by alleviating life stressors, increasing people's personal and social resources to enable them to use more and better coping strategies and influencing environmental forces so that they respond to people's needs. Practice must be sensitive to diversity, ethical and empowering, carried out through a partnership between worker and client that reduces power differences between them. Workers would come to shared agreement with clients about what issues are important, through listening to life stories and assessing in ways that allow clients to make informed choices about appropriate ways of responding. They would work in eight modalities: with individuals, families, groups, social networks, communities, physical environments, organisations and political action. Building up personal and collective strengths should be the main focus of action, which would emphasise clients taking decisions and action on their own account. The environment and the demands of the life course should be a constant factor in making decisions. Practice should be evaluated, and accumulated experience contributed to the professional knowledge base.

Three main phases are set out in Table 7.2.

Table 7.2. Germain and Gitterman's life model of practice

Phase	Helping process	Actions
Initial: beginnings	Auspice: create an accepting and supportive service environment	Demonstrate empathy in engaging with client: encourage client to express wishes and choices Describe service, agency and worker's role clearly Counteract effects of client group's experience of oppression
	Modalities	Select individual, family, group, community work according to client choice and type of life stressor
	Methods	Select episodic, emergency, short-term, time-limited open-ended service
	Skills	Assess person-environment for: • background: basic individual and family data • define life stressors • identify client expectations of worker and agency • client's strengths and limitations • physical environment Agree plans

Table 7.2 (cont.)

Phase	Helping process	Actions
Ongoing	Helping with stressful life transitions and traumatic events	Enable by demonstrating 'being alongside' client Explore and clarify issues by giving focus, direction, specifying issues, seeing patterns, offering hypotheses, encouraging reflection and feedback Mobilise strengths by identifying capacity, reassuring, offering hope Guide by providing and correcting information, offering advice and discussion, defining tasks Facilitate by identifying avoidance patterns, challenging false engagement, confronting inconsistencies
	Helping with environmental stressors	Identify role and structure of relevant social welfare agencies Identify supportive social networks Explore effect of physical environment: appropriate personal space, change semi-fixed space (moveable objects); mitigate effects of fixed space (building design) Coordinate and connect clients with organisational resources: collaborate with client, mediate with organisations Directive, assertive and persuasive interactions with organisations Adversarial or advocacy interactions with organisations
	Helping with family processes	Identify functions provided by family: procreation and socialisation of children; shelter; for protection of members; nurturing acceptance and self-realisation; connections to outside worlds Join the family group; affirm positives, track different life stories; create therapeutic contexts in which family can make progress; monitor family's paradigm (world view and structure) Interact with family; reframe perceptions, assign homework; work on rituals and patterns of behaviour; offer reflection
	Helping with group processes	Identify group focuses; education, problem-solving, specific behavioural change, carry out tasks, social purposes Identify internal stressors: problems in group formation, structural and value issues Form groups: gain organisational support, identify composition and structure, recruit members Offer support, identify needs for being different and separate, mediate between members
	Reducing interpersonal stress between worker and client	Identify sources of stress: agency authority and sanctions, worker authority and power, worker's professional socialisation, social differences, struggles for interpersonal control, taboo content Prepare effectively for likely issues; explore with interpersonal barriers openly
Termination endings	Auspice: organisational time and methods factors	Identify factors leading to ending in agency policy, timescale, and appropriate use of methods
	Relational factors	Changing client–worker relationship; differences in client or worker social background
	Phases	Identify and respond to negative feelings about ending and avoidance of ending Acknowledge sadness or pleasure at success; acknowledge release from responsibility of the work

Source: Germain and Gitterman (1996)

Analysis

The preparatory reading for this section will have reminded you how theory informs social work and how it is used to describe or explain practice, to articulate different approaches and values, to help us to understand issues or behaviours, and to help us reflect upon and develop professional practice. The extract above is from the same text and author. Here Payne presents Germain and Gitterman's life model of practice, but does not explore it specifically in the context of social work with older people. It is, however, provided here as an example of a model, based upon theory, which can be usefully critiqued and reflected upon in terms of its applicability to understanding the life course experiences of people in later adulthood. Therefore, as you read the extract, consider how coherently and thoroughly it explains the experience of later adulthood. Reflect back upon your reading of the JRF research project (earlier in this chapter) (Godfrey et al., 2004), and evaluate whether this model appears applicable and relevant given those findings. For example, Payne describes how the life model views the individual and their environment as *interdependent*. This would appear to correlate with some elements of the work of Godfrey et al. (2004), who highlighted the significance of communities, neighbours, mutual support and interdependence.

In the extract, Payne writes that, from the perspective of this model, *the aim of social work is to increase the **fit** between people and their environment* (2004, page 150, original emphasis). You may feel, on reading this sentence, that it is potentially a contentious statement in terms of social work practice. However, as you read the text further, this notion is explained and given more depth, and its alignment with the values and ethics of social work practice become very apparent. Thus Payne explains how, whilst the resources available to individuals are potentially constrained by social factors, social work practice can enable and empower individuals to strengthen their resources.

The table within this extract provides a useful breakdown of the model and makes the direct link to social work practice. The notion of a biographical approach, through listening to life stories, is embedded within the model and again reflects the reading and research articles that you have accessed earlier in this chapter.

Crawford and Walker (2003, page 18) outline a range of theories of human life course development: sociological, biological, psychosocial and psychological. This life model of practice is drawn broadly from a sociological perspective. It develops an ecological, systems theory approach, similar to the *Levels of action* shown in Figure 6.1.

As a practitioner in a social care environment, you may feel uncomfortable with a model or theory that puts so much emphasis on the impact of environmental or social issues, as these may detract from the conventional social work approach where the individual and their needs are paramount. This model could also be criticised for not considering the physical and biological changes in later adulthood and the impact that such changes may have upon the lives of individuals. However, the life model of practice, as explained in this extract, takes an holistic approach, listening to the individual and focusing on their experiences. In this way, the social work practice and intervention becomes centred on the older person and the areas of their life that they prioritise as being important:

In developing your understanding of later life, you should be mindful that an individual's life course development and life experiences are affected by a range of factors; these include social and economic aspects, cultural, historical, psychological, cognitive and physiological influences.

(Crawford and Walker, 2003, page 111)

Personal reflections

Reflect upon your own evaluation of Germain and Gitterman's life model for social work practice and whether you consider it valid and useful in helping you understand your own work with older people or the experiences of older people known to you. One way in which you might begin to be more specific in your analysis of their model would be to think of a particular older person known to you, and work through the *interpersonal resources* and the *social factors* listed by Payne, attempting to correlate these points with that older person's experience. You could then explore this model further by working through the table provided in the extract to appraise whether the helping processes and social work actions listed, through the phases of intervention with that older person, are realistic and valid in terms of contemporary social work practice. Given that Germain and Gitterman's model of practice was first developed in 1980 and was then published again in 1996, how relevant do you feel it is to modern day professional practice across the statutory, voluntary and independent sectors of social work provision?

Comment

In your reading and analysis of the extract you have worked through a brief critique of the life model. Your reflections, though, on putting specific elements of this model against your own practice experiences or your knowledge of particular individuals, may highlight particular weaknesses or strengths in the approach.

You will have formed a view about the relevance of this model to current day processes and practices in social work. A recent Audit Commission report *Supporting frail older people* (2004b) recommends that practice should be underpinned by a number of principles:

- increasing choice and control;
- proactively promoting health;
- adopting a whole-person approach, by exploring the whole range of issues that have an impact on older people's well-being, based on broad assessment processes;

and

- building a whole-system response, by ensuring that not just the NHS, but also social services, housing, the pension's service and a range of other agencies are appropriately involved.

(Audit Commission, 2004b, page 6–7)

Therefore, where social work practice incorporates these principles, no matter the setting or agency providing that service, it could be argued that the relevance of a sociologically based model is evident. Of course, it is always possible and arguably good practice to challenge, question and reflect upon the models and theories that underpin social work. In this way, you are developing your analytical skills, your knowledge and your own practice. You will also be more able to inform and support the practice of others.

Practical implications and activities

In this section of the chapter you have had an opportunity to reflect upon the use of theories and models in social work practice with people in later adulthood. The example used was particularly relevant to developing an understanding of the life course of individuals that you work with.

Following on from the comments above, and considering not only the particular example analysed here but also other models and theories familiar to you or used in your practice, make some notes in response to the following questions:

- how can your knowledge of social work theories and models, particularly those that help you to understand a life course perspective, change practice?
- how can you learn from these theories and develop your own practice?
- how can you apply these theories in practice and integrate your learning?

Chapter summary

In this chapter you have examined academic texts, research, theories and national policies in the context of life course development in later adulthood and social work practice. Firstly you explored constructions of later adulthood, analysing what research and knowledge evidence can tell us about how later adulthood is defined and understood, particularly by older people themselves. You then developed your understanding of the impact of transitions in later life, by looking at why it is important to understand how older people move through transitions, using retirement as an example of a transition. The last section of this chapter looked at ways in which theory can help to explain human development in later adulthood. Through an analysis of examples, you had the opportunity to explore how theories and models are used and how they can underpin social work practice.

As you have come to the end of the chapter, you are encouraged to reflect upon how you will develop and disseminate your learning further. In the next chapter there are some examples of ways in which you might go about this, depending upon your own learning needs at this stage in your professional development.

Annotated further reading and research

Arber, S, Davidson, K, Ginn, J (eds) (2003) *Gender and ageing: Changing roles and relationships*. Buckingham: Open University Press.

This book provides useful follow-up reading on each of the key topics covered in this chapter. Through an exploration of gender roles and relationships in later life, the authors explore changing identities, constructions of ageing and how transitions are experienced. In Chapter 3, for example, Eileen Fairhurst provides a wealth of qualitative data from focus group work with older people, which examines how people reconstruct their identities and relationships as they move through the transition of retirement. This chapter is, therefore, particularly relevant to the discussion on disengagement theory and retirement within this chapter. If you are not able to read through the whole text, you will find useful, short 'conclusions', which form summaries at the end of each chapter.

Walker, A and Hagan Hennessy, C (eds) (2004) *Growing older: Quality of life in old age*. Buckingham: Open University Press.

The twelve chapters of this edited text have been compiled by a number of academics and specialists in particular areas of health, social care and social gerontology. The book is particularly valuable because it offers short research-based summaries of the key findings from the work of the Economic and Social Research Council (ESRC) funded Growing Older Programme. Whilst the overall theme of the book is that of quality of life in later life, the breadth and range of topics covered include: ethnic inequalities; social support; frailty and institutional life; and environment, identity and old age. Furthermore, each chapter not only outlines the key findings of the research, but also addresses practice implications where relevant.

Age Concern England. **www.ageconcern.co.uk**

Age Concern is a federation of about 400 independent charities working together with and for older people, locally, regionally and nationally. On their website, you will find a wealth of information and research for students and for older people themselves and their carers. You will find that the section headed *Information and policy* is particularly helpful in providing statistical information, government policy, Age Concern commissioned research and links to a wide range of other related research organisations.

7 Developing as a reflective practitioner

ACHIEVING A SOCIAL WORK DEGREE

This chapter will begin to help you to meet the following National Occupational Standards:

Key Role 6: Demonstrate professional competence in social work practice.
- Research, analyse, evaluate, and use current knowledge of best social work practice.
- Work within agreed standards of social work practice and ensure own professional development.
- Contribute to the promotion of best social work practice.

It will also introduce you to the following academic standards as set out in the social work subject benchmark statement:

3.1.5 The nature of social work practice
- The processes of reflection and evaluation, including familiarity with the range of approaches for evaluating welfare outcomes, and their significance for the development of practice and the practitioner.

3.2.5 Skills in personal and professional development

Introduction

At key points throughout this book, you have been referred to this final chapter which aims to provide you with the context within which this reflective reader has been written, along with some ideas about ways in which you can use your studies of this book to promote your development as a reflective practitioner. Continuing learning and development is a feature of professional social work, both during studies towards the graduate qualification and post qualification. The requirement for social workers to continually improve their professional knowledge and skills is embedded in the codes of practice and within national policy standards, such as the national occupational standards; post registration training and learning requirements, and the post-qualifying framework.

Codes of practice

The *Codes of practice for social care workers and employers* describe the standards of professional conduct and practice within which social care workers and their employers should work. The codes have been developed by the General Social Care Council (GSCC) in order to assist in raising standards in social care services and are available from them at **www.gscc.org.uk**. The GSCC suggests that as a social worker or student social worker you use the codes to examine your own practice and to look for areas in which you can improve. The sixth code of practice in the document is particularly relevant to your responsibility to continually develop and reflect upon your practice. It is reproduced in the box below.

Extract from codes of practice for social care workers and employers

As a social care worker, you must be accountable for the quality of your work and take responsibility for maintaining and improving your knowledge and skills.

This includes:

6.1 Meeting relevant standards of practice and working in a lawful, safe and effective way;

6.2 Maintaining clear and accurate records as required by procedures established for your work;

6.3 Informing your employer or the appropriate authority about any personal difficulties that might affect your ability to do your job competently and safely;

6.4 Seeking assistance from your employer or the appropriate authority if you do not feel able or adequately prepared to carry out any aspect of your work, or you are not sure about how to proceed in a work matter;

6.5 Working openly and co-operatively with colleagues and treating them with respect;

6.6 Recognising that you remain responsible for the work that you have delegated to other workers;

6.7 Recognising and respecting the roles and expertise of workers from other agencies and working in partnership with them; and

6.8 Undertaking relevant training to maintain and improve your knowledge and skills and contributing to the learning and development of others.

www.gscc.org.uk

National Occupational Standards

The National Occupational Standards for social work describe the functions of social work and provide a standard of best practice in social work competence. All social work degree programmes in the United Kingdom are based upon these national standards, which provide the minimum standard that you should achieve on completion of a degree programme. The standards are available from the Sector Skills Council at **www.topssengland.net**. The codes of practice described above have been incorporated into the National Occupational Standards. The standards are divided into six key roles and whilst your learning across this book has significant relevance across each of the key roles, the requirement for social workers to take responsibility for their own practice and continuing development is encompassed within key roles 5 and 6. These are reproduced in the box below.

Extract from National Occupational Standards for social work

Key Role 5: **Manage and be accountable, with supervision and support, for your own social work practice within your organisation**

Unit 14 **Manage and be accountable for your own work**

14.1 Manage and prioritise your workload within organisational policies and priorities

14.2 Carry out duties using accountable professional judgement and knowledge-based social work practice

14.3	Monitor and evaluate the effectiveness of your programme of work in meeting the organisational requirements and the needs of individuals, families, carers, groups and communities
14.4	Use professional and managerial supervision and support to improve your practice
Unit 15	**Contribute to the management of resources and services**
Unit 16	**Manage, present and share records and reports**
16.1	Maintain accurate, complete, accessible, and up-to-date records and reports
16.2	Provide evidence for judgments and decisions
16.3	Implement legal and policy frameworks for access to records and reports
16.4	Share records with individuals, families, carers, groups and communities
Unit 17	**Work within multi-disciplinary and multi-organisational teams, networks and systems**
Key Role 6:	**Demonstrate professional competence in social work practice**
Unit 18	**Research, analyse, evaluate, and use current knowledge of best social work practice**
18.1	Review and update your own knowledge of legal, policy and procedural frameworks
18.2	Use professional and organisational supervision and support to research, critically analyse, and review knowledge based practice
18.3	Implement knowledge based social work models and methods to develop and improve your own practice
Unit 19	**Work within agreed standards of social work practice and ensure own professional development**
19.1	Exercise and justify professional judgments
19.2	Use professional assertiveness to justify decisions and uphold professional social work practice, values and ethics
19.3	Work within the principles and values underpinning social work practice
19.4	Critically reflect upon your own practice and performance using supervision and support systems
19.5	Use supervision and support to take action to meet continuing professional development needs
Unit 20	**Manage complex ethical issues, dilemmas and conflicts**
20.1	Identify and assess issues, dilemmas and conflicts that might affect your practice
20.2	Devise strategies to deal with ethical issues, dilemmas and conflicts
20.3	Reflect on outcomes
Unit 21	**Contribute to the promotion of best social work practice**
21.1	Contribute to policy review and development
21.2	Use supervision and organisational and professional systems to inform a course of action where practice falls below required standards
21.3	Work with colleagues to contribute to team development

Post-registration training and learning requirements (PRTL)

You may be an undergraduate student and feel that these requirements do not apply to you yet. However, as you will be responsible for evidencing continuing training and learning following initial qualification in order to maintain your registration, you should view this as a continuing element of your career path. Details of the requirements are available from the GSCC **www.gscc.org.uk** who state that:

- every social worker registered with the GSCC shall, within the period of registration, complete either 90 hours or 15 days of study, training, courses, seminars, reading, teaching or other activities which could reasonably be expected to advance the social worker's professional development, or contribute to the development of the profession as a whole; and
- every social worker registered with the GSCC shall keep a record of post-registration training and learning undertaken.

(**www.gscc.org.uk**)

Post-qualifying framework

Again, if you are an undergraduate student you may feel that this is not yet relevant to your studies. However, for qualified readers, the post-qualifying framework and the standards therein will be pertinent to your career planning and professional development. In the introduction to the framework, the GSCC explain how this post-qualifying framework *builds on the qualifying degree in social work*. The framework has three levels: specialist level, higher specialist level and advanced level. At each level the GSCC have provided generic level criteria which underpin any programmes of learning at that level. Within each of the generic level criteria there are criteria that stress critical reflection upon practice and continuing learning. Examples from the first level, specialist awards, have been extracted below.

Example of generic level criteria for post-qualifying awards in specialist social work.

- Think critically about their own practice in the context of the GSCC codes of practice, national and international codes of professional ethics and the principles of diversity, equity and social inclusion in a wide range of situations, including those associated with inter-agency and inter-professional work.
- Use reflection and critical analysis to continuously develop and improve their specialist practice, including their practice in inter-professional and inter-agency contexts, drawing systematically, accurately and appropriately on theories, models and relevant up-to-date research.
- Take responsibility for the effective use of supervision to identify and explore issues, develop and implement plans and improve own practice.

(GSCC, 2005)

Full details of the framework and the standards within it are available from the GSCC **www.gscc.org.uk**

This final section of the book is somewhat different to the chapters you have read so far, in that it aims to focus your reflective learning from this text so that you can demonstrate your ability to meet the standards and requirements that are applicable to your current situation. It is devoted to assisting you to identify ways in which you might progress your learning further, whilst ensuring that you keep a record of your progress and the impact this learning has had upon your professional development and social work practice. By the end of this chapter you will have had the opportunity to reflect upon how you can develop your studies further, both in terms of the areas you might explore and the types of study that you might undertake. You will also have looked at ways in which you can record and share your learning.

The rest of this chapter is therefore divided into short sections, each of which gives you suggestions and examples of ways in which you might progress your learning and record your progress. Brief reading extracts and reflective activities are incorporated into some of these sections.

Reflecting upon your own practice

This book is one in a series of social work education texts entitled *Reflective Readers*. Thus the emphasis on learning through reflection is to be expected. The two extracts below offer a summary of what is meant by reflection and what reflective learning can achieve.

Extract

Moon, J A (2004) *A handbook of reflective and experiental learning: Theory and practice*. London: RoutledgeFalmer. Pages 80–4.

The concept of reflection is represented by a number of different words that are in current parlance. We talk of 'reflection' itself, 'reflective learning', 'reflective writing' and 'reflective practice'. 'Reflection', as a process, seems to lie somewhere around the notion of learning and thinking. We reflect in order to learn something, or we learn as a result of reflecting – so 'reflective learning' as a term, simply emphasizes the intention to learn as a result of reflection. The content of 'reflective writing' is not a direct mirror of what happens in the head, but it is a representation of the process within a chosen medium – in this case, writing. The representation of reflection in the form of writing is likely to differ from that represented in other ways such as speech or in a drawing. In making a representation of personal reflection, we shape and model the content of our reflection in different ways and learn also from the process itself. In other words, there is secondary learning.

'Reflective practice' is a relatively new phrase that came into use particularly as a result of the work of Donald Schön (1983, 1987). Schön's first book was actually called *The Reflective Practitioner*. 'Reflective practice' emphasizes the use of reflection in professional or other complex activities as a means of coping with situations that are ill-structured and/or unpredictable. The idea of reflective practice was developed initially in nursing and teacher education and is increasingly being applied across the professions. It is, in essence, a professionalized form of 'reflective learning', but any kind of definition has remained problematic (Lyons, 1999).

On the basis of the reasoning above, we will be using the terms 'reflection' and 'reflective learning' interchangeably as the main terminology, recognizing that 'reflective writing' and 'reflective practice' represent expansions of the ideas in different directions and these terms will be used appropriately.

Some definitions of reflection and reflective learning

Moon (1999a) set out to clarify the nature of reflection, having observed the extraordinary complexity of the literature in this area. Some of the literature seems to suggest that reflection is no more than a form of thinking (the 'common-sense view of reflection', see below). However, that does not accord with the manner in which reflection is often operationalized in formal education (the academic view of reflection, see below). Enormously complicating the situation, too, is the literature from various disciplines, including education, professional development and psychology, that appears to use the idea of reflection in many different ways. The definitions have been refined and developed.

The common-sense view of reflection

The common-sense view of reflection is developed by examination of how we use the word 'reflection' in everyday language. We have said that reflection is akin to thinking but there is more to be added to this. We reflect usually in order to achieve an outcome, or for some purpose. We may, however, simply 'be reflective', and an outcome might then be unexpected. Reflection is an activity that we apply to more complex issues. We do not reflect on the route to the bus-stop, or on how to do a simple arithmetical sum where there is an obvious solution. We think it through or plan it. However, we might reflect on whether or not to complain about something when the complaint may generate difficult consequences. In addition, the content of reflection is largely what we know already. It is often a process of re-organizing knowledge and emotional orientations in order to achieve further insights.

On the basis of the reasoning above, a common-sense view of reflection can be stated as follows:

> Reflection is a form of mental processing – like a form of thinking – that we may use to fulfil a purpose or to achieve some anticipated outcome or we may simply 'be reflective' and then an outcome can be unexpected. Reflection is applied to relatively complicated, ill-structured ideas for which there is not an obvious solution and is largely based on the further processing of knowledge and understanding that we already possess.
>
> (based on, but extending the definition in Moon 1999a)

Reflection applied in academic contexts: a development of the common-sense view

Since the late 1990s, the theory and practice of reflection have attained a much more significant role in educational contexts. Unless there is clarity about the strictures that tend to be imposed upon reflection in these specific contexts, there is the danger that we will make an everyday activity technical. Reflection that is a requirement of a curriculum is likely to have some characteristics that are specified in advance. On this basis, it is useful to recognize a second view of reflection in order to encompass its application in the academic context. It would not be appropriate in academia, for example, to say that professional development is enhanced when a person goes for a sunny walk in a reflective mood. We would require something more tangible and directed – or the reflection might be expected to occur within a given structure. An element of the structure is likely to be a description of an incident. Furthermore, the outcome of reflection, which is most likely to be reflective writing, is usually seen by a tutor, and is often assessed. This can lead to some students writing the 'reflective' material that they think will be viewed favourably by their tutor (Salisbury, 1994). In addition, evidence of learning or change of behaviour may be expected to result from the process of reflection. These factors are also likely to influence the nature of reflective learning (Boud and Walker, 1998).

On the basis of the paragraph above, we can add to the common-sense definition of reflection as follows:

> Reflection/reflective learning or reflective writing in the academic context, is also likely to involve a conscious and stated purpose for the reflection, with an outcome specified in terms of learning, action or clarification. It may be preceded by a description of the purpose and/or the subject matter of the reflection. The process and outcome of reflective work are most likely to be in a represented (e.g., written) form, to be seen by others and to be assessed. All of these factors can influence its nature and quality.

In practice, the way in which reflection is used in educational situations is often quite narrowly defined. For example, it may be defined in terms of learning from recognized error or ineffectiveness in practice (Mackintosh, 1998; Hinnett, 2003) and it is often subject to some of the beliefs that are discussed later in this chapter. An example of such a belief is that reflection is always about the self.

Views of reflection that are focused on the outcomes of the process
As indicated above, much of the book *Reflection in Learning and Professional Development* (Moon, 1999a) was devoted to an exploration of how apparently different accounts of reflection in the literature could be describing the same basic process. It was observed that while accounts seemed to assume the common-sense view of reflection, their focus was on the ways in which reflection can be applied and how they produce a particular outcome rather than the mechanics of the process. This different focus seems to explain the diversity of the literature on reflection and the manner in which it has become complicated. From evidence of the literature, Moon suggests that the following outcomes can result from reflective processes:

- learning, knowledge and understanding;
- some form of action;
- a process of critical review;
- personal and continuing professional development;
- reflection on the process of learning or personal functioning (meta-cognition);
- the building of theory from observations in practice situations;
- the making of decisions/resolution of uncertainty, the solving of problems; empowerment and emancipation;
- unexpected outcomes (e.g., images, ideas that could be solutions to dilemmas or seen as creative activity);
- emotion (that can be an outcome or can be part of the process, see Chapter 3);
- clarification and the recognition that there is a need for further reflection.

(developed from Moon, 1999a, 1999b)

Although 'learning' (as above) is deemed to be an outcome of reflection in its own right, we could say that all the outcomes in the list are concerned with how we use understanding and knowledge to achieve other purposes. In other words, these factors link reflection with the process of learning.

In these short extracts from Moon's work it is clear that, whatever terminology is chosen, the processes of reflection and the outcomes thereof can result in the acquisition of knowledge and understanding. Thus, since the 1990s, reflective social work practice has become ever more significant, particularly when considering the interface between theory and practice (Payne 2002, page 123).

Having acknowledged the value and outcomes from effective reflective practice you need to consider the practical steps that you will take in order to develop your own reflective practice. You may be familiar with Kolb's cycle of experiential learning (Kolb, 1984), in which learning is explained as taking place through a cyclical process of reflecting upon and conceptualising an experience; hypothesising about how to learn or practice differently following that reflection; then trying out the revised practice, upon which the process of reflection is again founded. In other words, Kolb sees experience being translated, through reflection, into learning and potentially improved practice. Using Kolb's model it is possible to connect these different stages of the cycle with practical actions that you might engage in at each stage. The diagram below illustrates some examples of reflective activities that can be associated with the different stages of Kolb's learning cycle.

The examples in the illustration are broad and are only examples. More specifically, in respect of work with services users and carers and the life course perspective explored in this book, as you talk and listen to people, reflect upon what they are telling you. Listen to their life biographies, how they interpret and narrate their own lives and situations, how they express the things that are important to them and the concerns that they have. You should then think critically about your own values and actions, analysing and reflecting upon your practice with individual service-users. Work through, in your own mind, what you did, why you did it that way, what was effective or less effective and how you might improve on your practice for the future.

As has been suggested, you should use your peers and managers as mentors, advisors and supporters, for example using both formal and informal social work supervision as vehicles for reflection and learning. Where appropriate, at the right time, you could ask service-users and carers how they experienced your intervention in their lives. This would give you further ideas to reflect on.

During many social work undergraduate and post-graduate learning programmes, you will be required to keep a reflective diary or journal providing reflective commentaries on your practice. It is good practice for all practitioners to record reflective commentaries to inform their practice, not only those who are undertaking formal programmes of learning. Moon (2004) offers many helpful suggestions of ways in which reflective writing can be developed to ensure it is effective in supporting and enhancing the depth of your learning.

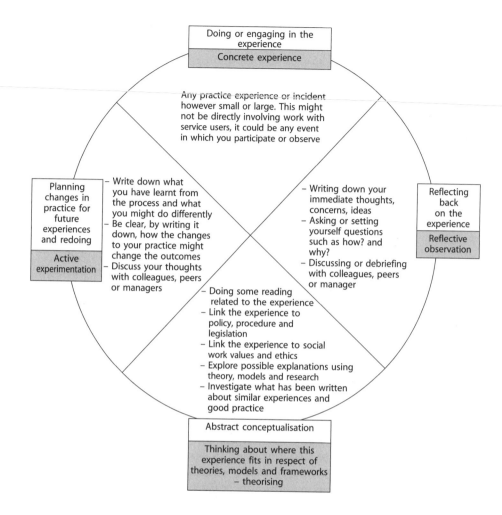

Figure 7.1 Examples of practical reflective practice activities associated
with Kolb's experiential learning cycle

Activity

Whether you are a social work practitioner, a full-time student, or are combining
both studies and social care practice, think about the ways in which you appraise
your own practice. In other words think about the different methods and processes
that help you to evaluate your own social work practice. Make some notes in
response to the questions below:

- how do you know you are doing a good job?
- what strategies do you have to evaluate your efforts?
- where do you gather information from to inform your self-appraisal? Is this
  formal or informal?

Comment

You may have identified a number of ways in which you receive feedback about your practice, perhaps including formal organisational processes of supervision and regular line-manager appraisal. As a student, you may also have taken account of assessment feedback and practice assessor comments. Additionally, you may have included something about personal reflections on practice as another element of evaluation, namely a form of self-appraisal. A further source of feedback on practice is service-user and carer comments and potentially peer observations of practice or peer feedback. As an extension of this exercise, think about ways in which you could record your self-appraisal and reflections, as such records would provide a further mechanism for future evaluation of further development.

Extending your reading and studying further

Throughout the book, I have frequently recommended that you undertake a search of additional current legislation and guidance that supports the particular aspect of social work practice that you are learning about. You could then consider whether a life course perspective has underpinned the content of the documents you locate and how your work to implement national requirements can be informed by your knowledge of human life course development. Furthermore, accessing the additional areas of reading suggested at the end of each chapter, reading and analysing other research, texts and journal articles will support your continued learning in this area.

As well as putting your practice and learning into the national context, you should ensure that you develop your understanding of the context of your specific practice setting, for example, examining particular processes and procedures used in your agency and area of practice. A specific example might be the type of assessment that you use, for example, the *Single Assessment*. You could critique this process against your knowledge of transitions and life course development in later adulthood, for example, making notes as you consider how it enables you to take account of the whole of people's lives and their own perspectives on it.

You may also have a particular interest in one area of social work, for example young people who misuse substances or older people who have a learning disability, or adults from particular cultural backgrounds. If this is so, it would be useful and relevant for you to look in more depth at how a life course perspective can inform this particular specialist area of work.

Developing as a knowledge/evidence-informed practitioner

Throughout this book you have been presented with a range of different knowledge, which has been extracted from research, policy documents, legislation and academic texts. You have been encouraged and assisted to link this knowledge to your practice, whilst also critically evaluating the different data by questioning, making comparisons, looking for links to other literature and taking an overall critical viewpoint.

This approach, commonly called evidence-based practice, is defined as *the conscientious, explicit and judicious use of current best evidence in making decisions regarding the welfare of those in need* (Sheldon cited in Smith, 2004, page 8). However, the term knowledge informed practice can be seen to be more inclusive, encompassing the use of a range of knowledge. The Social Care Institute for Excellence (SCIE) (2004) in a *knowledge review* identifies five different types of knowledge applicable to the development of social care.

1. *Organisational knowledge* – this relates to regulations and knowledge that arises from organising quality social care.
2. *Practitioner knowledge* – knowledge gained from experience and is said to be both personal and context-specific.
3. *User knowledge* – knowledge gained from the experience of using social care services.
4. *Research knowledge* – evidence from systematic, empirical research findings.
5. *Policy community knowledge* – gained from the wider policy and strategy context.

(Walter et al., 2004, p viii)

Activity

Reflect back upon your learning across this book and perhaps taking one chapter at a time, attempt to categorise the knowledge that is located within the pre-reading and the extracts, according to the categories given above. Read through the following questions and make a note of your responses:

- Are there any categories that are less well represented in the book? If so, how will you gain that form of knowledge in relation to human life course development and your particular practice interests?
- When you are working in practice, either as a student or as a qualified worker, which of these areas of knowledge inform your practice?

Comment

I suspect that you will concur that much of the knowledge evidence produced in this book, through the extracts and pre-reading, falls into the latter three categories. If you agree, then it would be *organisational knowledge* and *practitioner knowledge* that you need to look to enhance. I would suggest that the whole book and, in particular, this chapter, offer suggestions of ways in which you can begin to develop your practitioner knowledge. Additionally, earlier in this chapter, when looking at extending your studies, the importance of developing your understanding in the context of particular processes and procedures used in your agency and area of practice was considered. This is the way in which you will enhance your organisational knowledge.

Undertaking practitioner research

The potential for practitioner research in social care may be under-developed (Shaw and Lishman, 1999; Statham, 2004), but it remains a valued method of learning and continuing professional development. After all, as Statham (2004, page 161) reminds us, when practitioners find procedures and structures imposed on their practice, which they feel are not helpful or relevant, they will quickly ask why they were not involved in the development process. Practitioner research need not be large scale or very grand and can be undertaken alone or in small groups. If you are studying at either undergraduate or post graduate levels, it is very likely that your programme will include modules that have elements of research and investigation within them. If you are working in practice, you could consider, as part of your professional development plan and as a way of increasing your understanding about your own practice, investigating a discrete area of practice that interests you. Details of the *Research in practice* organisation are given at the end of this chapter and you are advised to look at the support that they provide, which includes, for example, a step-by-step guide to conducting a survey.

Activity

Whether you are a social work practitioner, a full-time student, or are combining both studies and social care practice, think about the ways in which you might become involved in practitioner research.

- What might be the key research questions that you would be interested to investigate?
- How would you design research to most effectively research those questions?

Disseminating and sharing your learning

Wenger (1998) describes learning as a process of engagement in shared practice, through which meanings are negotiated and identities developed in *communities of practice*. You may belong to and interact with a number of communities of practice and it is within these social learning structures that you can disseminate, share and reflect on your own learning. For example, when you have worked through the *personal reflections* and the *practical activities* sections in each chapter, you could find ways of sharing your learning or discussing your thoughts with colleagues, for example other students or other practitioners. You might talk with your peers in a team setting, or in a multidisciplinary setting, perhaps with medical and nursing staff. It would be very useful to compare and contrast the different ideas that might come forward.

Recording your learning and the activities you undertake

In this chapter, you have been reading about ways in which you could continue to reflect, expand upon your learning and develop your professional practice. It is strongly recommended that, as you undertake any of the above activities, or other opportunities for learning offered in this book, you also record your learning. There are different ways in which you might do this, perhaps using a reflective log, as discussed earlier, or keeping a portfolio of learning. If you are registered as a social worker with the General Social Care Council (GSCC) (**www.gscc.org.uk**) then you are required to undertake post-registration training and learning (PRTL). The GSCC provide, on their website and in registration packs, a suggested format to keep a record of PRTL activities that you undertake. The format of this *Record of achievement* is reproduced in Figure 7.2.

Date	Duration	Details of training and learning activity (including name of provider of training and learning activity)	State how this has contributed to your training and learning
Total training and learning for period of registration			Hours: Days:

Figure 7.2 Format of GSCC record of achievement document to record post-registration training and learning activities

You will notice, though, that this format is, exactly as it says, a record of your training and learning activities. It does not therefore include space for evidence of development or reflective journaling. I would recommend, therefore, as well as keeping an overall log of training and learning that you have undertaken, whether this is pre- or post-qualification, that you also maintain a portfolio of evidence that can be cross-referenced to that record. This should include your experiences of supporting, teaching or mentoring others and the times when you disseminate or share your learning.

As an example, your reading and work on the chapters in this book will provide evidence of that learning as it will advance your professional development, but you must keep a record of that learning. As a minimum, it is recommended that you record the date, the amount of time that you worked on the chapter and/or the various activities, and the learning that you achieved through this. You could write a short reflective summary of your perspectives on the outcomes of your studies. In order to structure your summaries as you use this reflective reader, it is suggested that you could address the following questions as you complete each chapter:

- what do I know, or can I do now, that I did not know or could not do before I did this section of studying?
- is there anything I did not understand or want to explore further?
- what else do I need to know to extend my professional development and learning in this area?

Constructing a career development plan

During this chapter, I have mentioned the concept of a career plan. You may have very clear ideas about your future professional development, or you may be less focused on your future aspirations. However, you will find that the process of thinking through and planning your short-, medium- and long-term professional goals can be very helpful in assisting you to decide upon the focus of your learning and development activities, whether this is during your undergraduate studies, or at post-qualifying level.

Activity

Make a list of the things you want to achieve in your professional working life and how you aim to achieve them. Then prioritise that list and attempt to give each aim a realistic timeframe. Finally, go back through each of your professional aims and make a note of your learning needs in respect of each aim and the resources that you will need in order to fulfil that aim. This is the beginnings of a career development plan which you may wish to discuss further with your colleagues, peers, tutor or line-manager.

Comment

It is, of course, not possible for me to know what each reader's professional career plan might look like. However, this process requires you to reflect upon where you are now and the skills that you already have, and to look forward to where you want to be and the skills that you need to develop. Once you have written a career development plan in this way, even though it may change as you learn and are exposed to new experiences, you will have a baseline against which you can review your progress.

Conclusion

In this final chapter of this reflective reader you have focused on thinking about ways in which you can reflect upon your learning from the other six chapters of the book and take that learning forward in your practice. The chapter started by demonstrating how continuing development and updating of professional practice, through, for example, reflective learning, is emphasised within the national social work professional standards and requirements. Thereafter, you explored a number of different ways in which you might extend, deepen, disseminate and record your learning. You may feel prepared, or in an appropriate situation, to progress only some of the ideas in this chapter at this time. Thus it is recommended that you give consideration to your learning needs and preferred style of learning as you test out some of the options suggested here. You should also identify the person, or people, for example your peers, manager, mentor or tutor, who will support and enable your learning and enlist their help and advice as you progress.

Annotated further reading and research

Moon, J A (2004) *A handbook of reflective and experiential learning: Theory and practice.* London: RoutledgeFalmer.
This contemporary book provides a very comprehensible text that explores how knowledge is acquired and learning takes place through experience and reflection. The final section of the book may be of particular interest to students at all levels, as the author provides a range of reflective activities and guidance in the process of writing reflectively.

Research in Practice (RiP). **www.rip.org.uk**
Research in Practice is a research implementation collaborative organisation which has over 80 participating agencies in the United Kingdom. Their mission, according to their website, is to *promote positive outcomes for children and families through the use of research evidence.* The website has a substantial amount of very useful information for practitioners including publications, a searchable 'evidence bank' and a section about forthcoming learning events.

Research in Practice for Adults. (RiPfA) **www.ripfa.org.uk**
Research in Practice for Adults is a newly established organisation which mirrors the structural organisation of the Research in Practice project detailed above. The mission of RiPfA is *to promote the use of evidence-informed practice in the planning and delivery of adult social care services*. Their website provides an abundance of resources for practitioners working with adults and who want to develop a more knowledgeable or an evidence-informed approach to their practice.

References

Abbott, L and Langston, A (eds) (2004) *Birth to three matters.* Buckingham: Open University Press.

Age Concern Policy Papers (2005) *Interested in ageing? Older people's lives: Key issues and evidence,* Ref 0905. London: Age Concern.

Aldgate, J (2006) Children, development and ecology, in Aldgate, J, Jones, D, Rose, W and Jeffery, C (eds) *The developing world of the child,* pages 17–34. London: Jessica Kingsley.

Arber, S, Davidson K and Ginn, J (eds) (2003) *Gender and ageing: Changing roles and relationships.* Buckingham: Open University Press.

Arnold, C (1999) *Child development and learning 2–5 years: Georgia's story.* London: Hodder & Stoughton.

Audit Commission (2004a) *Older people – building a strategic approach.* London: Audit Commission.

Audit Commission (2004b) *Supporting frail older people – independence and well-being 3.* London: Audit Commission.

Barnes, H and Parry, J (2003) *Renegotiating identity and relationships: Men and women's adjustments to retirement.* London: Policy Studies Institute.

Beckett, C (2002) *Human growth and development.* London: Sage.

Beckett, C and Maynard, A (2005) *Values and ethics in social work.* London: Sage.

Bee, H and Bjorklund, B (2004) *The journey of adulthood.* 5th edn. New Jersey: Pearson Education.

Bell, J (1999) *Doing your research project: A guide for first-time researchers in education and social science.* 3rd edn. Maidenhead: Open University Press.

Berryman, J C, Smythe, P K, Taylor, A, Lamont, A and Joiner, R (2002) *Developmental psychology and you.* 2nd edn. Oxford: Blackwell.

Bodrova, E and Leong, D (2003) The importance of being playful. *Educational leadership,* 60 (7), 50–3.

Brewster, J and Ramcharan, P (2005) Enabling and supporting person-centred approaches in Grant, G, Goward, P, Richardson, M and Ramcharan, P (eds) *Learning Disability: A Life Cycle Approach to Valuing People.* Buckingham: Open University Press.

Burnett, R and Roberts, C (eds) (2004) *What works in probation and youth justice: Developing evidence-based practice.* Cullompton: Willan Publishing.

Bynner, J, Elias, P, McKnight, A, Pan, H and Pierre, G (2002) *Young people's changing routes to independence.* York: YPS for the Joseph Rowntree Foundation.

Cabinet Office (2005) *Improving the life chances of disabled people – final report.* London: HMSO. **www.strategy.gov.uk**

Calder, A and Cope, R (2003) *Breaking barriers? Reaching the hardest to reach.* London: The Prince's Trust.

Case, S and Haines, K (2004) Promoting prevention: Evaluating a multi-agency initiative of youth consultation and crime prevention in Swansea. *Children and society*, 18 (5), 355–70.

Connexions Direct – Information and advice for young people. **www.connexions-direct.com**

Crawford, K and Walker, J (2003) *Social work and human development.* Exeter: Learning Matters.

Crawford, K and Walker, J (2004) *Social work with older people.* Exeter: Learning Matters.

Currer, C (1991) Understanding the mother's viewpoint: The case of Pathan women in Britain, in Wyke, S and Hewison, J (eds) *Child health matters: Caring for children in the community.* Buckingham: Open University Press.

Dalrymple, J (2005) Constructions of child and youth advocacy: Emerging issues in advocacy practice. *Children and society,* 19, 3–15.

Daniel, B, Wassell, S and Gilligan, R (1999) *Child development for child care and protection workers.* London: Jessica Kingsley.

Department for Education and Skills (DfES) (2001) *Learning to listen: Core principles for the involvement of children and young people.* Nottingham: DfES Publications Centre. **www.everychildmatters.gov.uk/participation**

Department for Education and Skills (DfES) (2002) *Birth to three matters: A framework to support children in their earliest years.* Nottingham: DfES Publications Centre. **www.surestart.gov.uk**

Department for Education and Skills (DfES) (2003) *Every child matters*, Cm5860. London: The Stationery Office. **www.dfes.gov.uk**

Department for Education and Skills (DfES) (2004) *Every child matters: Change for children.* London: The Stationery Office. **www.everychildmatters.gov.uk**

Department for Education and Skills (DfES) (2005) *Youth matters*, Cm6629. London: The Stationery Office. **www.dfes.gov.uk**

Department for Education and Skills (DfES) (2005a) *Common core of skills and knowledge for the children's workforce.* Nottingham: DfES Publications Centre. **www.dfes.gov.uk/commoncore**

Department for Education and Skills (DfES) (2006) *The Common Assessment Framework for children and young people: Practitioners' guide.* **www.everychildmatters.gov.uk/caf**

Department of Health (DoH) (1995) *Child protection: Messages from research.* London: HMSO.

Department of Health (DoH) (1999) *Working together to safeguard children.* London: The Stationery Office.

Department of Health (DoH) (2001) *Assessing children in need and their families: Practice guidelines.* London: The Stationery Office. **www.wales.gov.uk**

Department of Health (DoH) (2001a) *The Children Act now: Messages from research.* London: HMSO.

Department of Health (DoH) (2001b) *The National Service Framework for older people.* London: The Stationery Office. **www.doh.gov.uk/nsf/olderpeople.htm**

Department of Health (DoH) (2001c) *Valuing people – a new strategy for learning disability for the 21st century*, Cm5086. London: The Stationery Office. **www.doh.gov.uk**

Department of Health (DoH) (2002) *Listening, hearing and responding.* London: The Stationery Office. **www.doh.gov.uk**

Department of Health (DoH) (2004) *National Service Framework for children, young people and maternity services.* London: The Stationery Office. **www.doh.gov.uk**

Department of Health (DoH) (2005) *Independence, well-being and choice: Our vision for the future of social care for adults in England*, Cm6499. London: The Stationery Office. **www.doh.gov.uk**

Department of Health (DoH) (2006) *Our health, our care, our say: A new direction for community services*, Cm6737. Norwich: The Stationery Office. **www.dh.gov.uk/publications**

Dowling, M, Gupta, A and Aldgate, J (2006) The impact of community and environmental factors, in Aldgate, J, Jones, D, Rose, W and Jeffery, C (eds) *The developing world of the child,* pages 141–60. London: Jessica Kingsley.

Eamon, M K (2001) The effects of poverty on children's socioemotional development : An ecological systems analysis. *Social Work*, 46 (3), 256–66.

Erikson, E H (1995) *A way of looking at things: Selected papers from 1930 to 1980.* London: Norton and Co.

Fairhurst, E (2005) New identities in ageing: Perspectives on age, gender and life after work, in Arber, S, Davidson, K, Ginn, J (2003) *Gender and ageing: Changing roles and relationships.* Buckingham: Open University Press.

General Social Care Council (GSCC) (2002) *Codes of practice for social care workers and employers.* London: GSCC. **www.gscc.org.uk**

General Social Care Council (GSCC) (2005) *Post-qualifying framework for social work education and training.* London: GSCC. **www.gscc.org.uk**

Gillies, V (2000) Young people and family life: Analysing and comparing disciplinary discourses. *Journal of youth studies*, 3 (2), 211–28.

Godfrey, M, Townsend, J and Denby, T (2004) *Building a good life for older people in local communities: The experience of ageing in time and place*, Ref 041. York: Joseph Rowntree Foundation. **www.jrf.org.uk**

Grant, G, Goward, P, Richardson, M and Ramcharan, P (eds) (2005) *Learning disability: A life cycle approach to valuing people.* Buckingham: Open University Press.

Grewal, I, McManus, S, Arthur, S and Reith, L (2004) *Making the transition: Addressing barriers in services for disabled people.* Leeds: Corporate Document Services. **www.dwp.gov.uk**

Gubrium, J and Holstein, J (eds) (2003) *Ways of aging.* Oxford: Blackwell.

Haines, K and Case, S (2004) *Extending entitlement: Making it real.* Cardiff: Welsh Assembly Government.

Hawkins, JD and Catalano, RF (1992) *Communities that care.* San Francisco, CA: Jossey Bass.

Healthcare Commission (2006) *Living well in later life: A review of progress against the National Service Framework for older people.* London: Commission for Healthcare Audit and Inspection.

HM Treasury (2004) *Child poverty review.* London: The Stationery Office. **www-hm-treasury.gov.uk**

Hockey, J and James, A (2003) *Social identities across the life course.* Basingstoke: Palgrave Macmillan.

Hood, R (2004) Foreword, in Burnett, R and Roberts, C *What works in probation and youth justice: Developing evidence-based practice.* Cullompton: Willan Publishing.

Hunt, S (2005) *The life course: A sociological introduction.* Basingstoke: Palgrave Macmillan.

James, A and James, A L (2004) *Constructing childhood: Theory, policy and social practice.* Basingstoke: Palgrave Macmillan.

James, A, Jenks, C and Prout, A (1998) *Theorizing childhood.* Cambridge: Polity Press.

Jones, G (2002) *The youth divide: Diverging paths to adulthood.* York: Joseph Rowntree Foundation. **www.jrf.org.uk**

Jowitt, M and O'Loughlin, S (2005) *Social work with children and families.* Exeter: Learning Matters.

Kolb, D (1984) *Experiential learning as the science of learning and development.* New Jersey: Prentice-Hall.

Laming, H (2003) *The Victoria Climbié inquiry report,* Cm5730. London: The Stationery Office. **www.victoria-climbie-inquiry.org.uk**

Mayall, B (2000) Conversations with children: Working with generational issues, in Christensen, P and James, A (eds) *Research with children: Perspectives and practices,* pages 120–35. London: RoutledgeFalmer.

Mills, C (2004) *Problems at home, problems at school: The effects of maltreatment in the home on children's functioning at school: An overview of recent research.* London: NSPCC.

Mir, G, Nocon, A and Ahmad, W with Jones L (2001) *Learning difficulties and ethnicity: Report to the Department of Health.* London: Department of Health. **www.doh.gov/ukxira.htm**

Moon, J A (2004) *A handbook of reflective and experiential learning: Theory and practice.* London: RoutledgeFalmer.

Morrison, M (2002) What do we mean by educational research?, in Coleman, M and Briggs, A (eds) (2002) *Research methods in educational leadership and management.* London: Paul Chapman Publishing.

Morrow, V and Richards, M (1996) The ethics of social research with children. *Children and society,* 10 (2), 90–105.

Morss, J R (2002) The several social constructions of James, Jenks and Prout: A contribution to the sociological theorization of childhood. *The international journal of children's rights,* 10, 39–54.

National Assembly for Wales, Department for Training and Education (2000) *Extending entitlement: Supporting young people in Wales.* Cardiff: Welsh Assembly Government. **www.wales.gov.uk/youngpeople**

National Office for Statistics **www.statistics.gov.uk/census2001**

O'Hagan, K (1999) Culture, cultural identity, and cultural sensitivity in child and family social work. *Child and family social work*, 4, 269–81.

Oliver, M (1990) *The politics of disablement.* Basingstoke: Macmillan.

Oliver, M (1996) Defining impairment and disability, in Barnes, C and Mercer, G (eds) *Exploring the divide: Illness and disability.* Leeds: Disability Press.

Paludi, M A (2002) *Human development in multicultural contexts: A book of readings.* New Jersey: Prentice-Hall.

Parker, J and Bradley, G (2003) *Social work practice: Assessment, planning, intervention and review.* Exeter: Learning Matters.

Payne, M (2002) Social work theories and reflective practice, in Adams, R, Dominelli, L and Payne, M *Social work: Themes, issues and critical debates.* 2nd edn. Basingstoke: Palgrave Macmillan.

Payne, M (2005) *Modern social work theory.* 3rd edn. Basingstoke: Palgrave Macmillan.

Phillipson, C (1998) *Reconstructing old age.* London: Sage.

Priestley, M (2000) Adults only: Disability, social policy and the life course. *Journal of social policy*, 29 (2), 421–39.

Quinton, D (2006) Self-development, in Aldgate, J, Jones, D, Rose, W and Jeffery, C (eds) *The developing world of the child*, pages 97–111. London: Jessica Kingsley.

Russell, IM (2005) *A national framework for youth action and engagement.* Norwich: HMSO.

Schofield, G (2006) Middle childhood: Five to eleven years, in Aldgate, J, Jones, D, Rose, W and Jeffery, C (eds) *The developing world of the child*, pages 196–207. London: Jessica Kingsley.

Seden, J (2006) Frameworks and theories, in Aldgate, J, Jones, D, Rose, W and Jeffery, C (eds) *The developing world of the child*, pages 35–54. London: Jessica Kingsley.

Shaw, I and Lishman, J (1999) *Evaluation and social work practice.* London: Sage.

Sheridan, MD (1975) *From birth to five years: Children's developmental progress.* 3rd edn. London: Routledge.

Smith, D (ed) (2004) *Social work and evidence-based practice.* London: Jessica Kingsley.

Social Policy Research Unit (SPRU) (2005) *Outcomes for disabled service users.* York: University of York SPRU.

Statham, D (ed) (2004) *Managing front line practice in social care.* London: Jessica Kingsley.

Sugarman, L (2001) *Life-span development: Frameworks, accounts and strategies.* Hove: Psychology Press Ltd.

Vaillant, GE (1977) *Adaptation to life: How the best and brightest come of age.* Boston, MA: Linde Brown.

Walker, A and Hagan Hennessy, C (eds) (2004) *Growing older: Quality of life in old age.* Buckingham: Open University Press.

Walter, I, Nutley, S, Percy-Smith, J, McNeish, D and Frost, S (2004) *Improving the use of research in social care practice.* London: Social Care Institute for Excellence (SCIE).

Wenger, E (1998) *Communities of practice: Learning, meaning and identity.* Cambridge: Cambridge University Press.

Williams, A (2005) New developments in care planning for children in residential care, in Crimmens, D and Milligan, I (eds) *Facing forward: Residential child care in the 21st century.* Lyme Regis: Russell House Publishing.

Wood, D (1998) *How children think and learn.* 2nd edn. Oxford: Blackwell.

Woodhead, M and Montgomery, H (2003) *Understanding childhood: an interdisciplinary approach.* Chichester: Wiley and Sons Ltd.

Glossary of terms

Advocacy

There is a range of ways in which advocacy is interpreted. Advocacy in the context of this book and the enabling professions relates to the work of individuals, who may be paid or unpaid, who help to express and articulate the wishes and feelings of another person. They may speak up for and support that person to interpret and present their views. Thus advocacy, through the work of advocates, helps individuals to represent their interests, gain their rights and express their opinions.

Ageism

Where negative generalisations, assumptions or stereotypes result in people being treated unfairly, or discriminated against, because of their age.

Attachment

'... a positive emotional link between two people – a link of affection' (Lindon, cited in Crawford and Walker, 2003: 43)

Attachment theory

Theory that explains the significance of attachment and relationships, in particular the bonds between children and care-givers.

Continuing professional development (CPD)

Continuing professional development is the systematic maintenance and improvement of knowledge, skills and competence, and enhancement of learning, undertaken by a person throughout his or her working life. (Institute of Continuing Professional Development **www.cpdinstitute.org**)

Department for Education and Skills (DfES)

The Department for Education and Skills whose stated purpose is to create opportunity, release potential and achieve excellence for all. **www.dfes.gov.uk**

Department of Health (DoH)

Government Department that provides health and social care policy, guidance and publications. **www.dh.gov.uk**

Developmental

Relating to growth, progression and advancement.

Developmental pathways
Development trajectories

Both these terms relate to the different courses or routes, through a range of experiences and transitions, that individuals may take as they grow and progress through the life course.

Disengagement theory

A theory built on the premise that withdrawal from social participation and interaction is an expected and natural process in later adulthood. Disengagement and detachment is perceived as positive and normal for older people. This perspective is examined in detail in Chapter 6 of this text.

Ecological

Relating to the environment in which people live.

General Social Care (GSCC) www.gscc.org.uk

The workforce regulator and guardian of Council standards for the social care workforce in England. They were established in October 2001 under the Care Standards Act 2000. They are responsible for the codes of practice, Social Care Register and social work education and training.

Generativity

A concept that relates to *generating* or being productive and contributing in some way to future society. This is discussed in detail in Chapter 5 of this text.

Holistic

An approach that focuses on the whole of something, in the case of social work, this would usually be the whole of the person's life and current circumstances, and not just one element. Holistic approaches view the different aspects of a person as being closely interconnected and understandable only by reference to the whole.

Identity development

A process of forming an awareness of 'who we are'. Understanding ourselves as a person, developing personality and a concept of self in relation to others in the social world. Becoming conscious and confident about one's personal life history, sexuality, race, gender and ethnicity.

Life course

The progression and path an individual takes from conception to death (Crawford and Walker, 2003, page 3).

Life course perspective

A viewpoint that considers the whole of a life (from conception to death) as offering opportunities for growth, development and change. (Crawford and Walker, 2003, page 3). This perspective is defined in more detail in Chapter 1 of this book.

Milestones

Expected stages of sequential development of skills and abilities, usually in children and commonly related to age. These stages are based upon that which is deemed *normal* and are used to gauge children's development and identify potential developmental problems.

National Service Framework (NSF)

The national service frameworks are national strategies which set out goals and programmes for change within specific areas of health and social care. The National Service Frameworks for Children (2004) and Older People (2001) are particularly pertinent to this reflective reader.

Narrative or biographical

The narrative approach is a *way of working approach with individuals that focuses on the importance of their own first-hand account of their life, their experiences and the meaning they attach to them* (Crawford and Walker, 2003, page 3). The narrative approach is defined in more detail in Chapter 1 of this book.

Post-registration training and learning (PRTL)
This is the term used by the GSCC and is taken here to mean the activities that individuals may undertake in order to achieve Continuing Professional Development (CPD).

Psychosocial theories
Theories that arise from aspects of both sociological and psychological perspectives.

Puberty
A stage of human development which is defined by biological, physical change – the reproductive organs, in males and females, become functional.

Transition
Phases, stages or life events that people move through during their life course.

Social construction
Where a common understanding or meaning of a concept is taken for granted, so that the notion appears to be obvious to those who accept it. However, the meaning actually emerges from ideologies, images, values and beliefs in a particular culture or society.

A systems perspective
A theoretical stance that views individuals as part of social systems that are dynamic and interconnected. This perspective focuses on the interaction and relationships between people and their environment.

Index